'Ndrangheta

Anna Sergi • Anita Lavorgna

'Ndrangheta

The Glocal Dimensions of the Most Powerful Italian Mafia

Anna Sergi
Department of Sociology
University of Essex
Colchester, United Kingdom

Anita Lavorgna
Department of Sociology
Social Policy and Criminology
University of Southampton
Southampton, United Kingdom

ISBN 978-3-319-32584-2   ISBN 978-3-319-32585-9   (eBook)
DOI 10.1007/978-3-319-32585-9

Library of Congress Control Number: 2016945984

Cover illustration: © Stephen Bonk / Fotolia.co.uk

Printed on acid-free paper

This Palgrave Macmillan imprint is published by Springer Nature
The registered company is Springer International Publishing AG Switzerland

ACKNOWLEDGEMENTS

The authors would like to thank the Antimafia District Directorate (DDA) in Catanzaro (especially Antimafia Prosecutor Giovanni Bombardieri) and in Reggio Calabria (especially Antimafia Prosecutor Roberto Di Palma) for their support in gathering judicial files and arranging interviews for this book.

The Authors are also thankful to Connie Agius (freelance journalist) and Carlo Macrì (correspondent for *Il Corriere della Sera*) for their expertise and support in gathering data related to judicial operations.

Finally, the Authors wish to thank Pantaleone Sergi, President of the ICSAIC – Centro di Ricerca sulle Migrazioni, at the University of Calabria, for his support in gathering migration figures and for granting access to the centre's historical archives.

ACKNOWLEDGMENTS

Contents

LIST OF FIGURES

CHAPTER 1

Introduction

Abstract The introduction of this book will present the scope of our analysis: the Calabrian region, and the Calabrian mafia, the 'ndrangheta. It will offer the outline of the book, discuss the choice of the title, and explain the rationale of our choices in terms of structure of the chapters and conceptualisation of the phenomena we are going to describe and analyse. It will also explain our theoretical approach to mafia-type organised crime as behavioural model and justify it by presenting the main approaches to mafias in Italy and the peculiarities of the Calabrian 'ndrangheta. Finally, the chapter will offer a brief presentation of the geography of the Calabrian region.

Keywords 'Ndrangheta • Calabrian Mafia • 'Ndranghetisation • 'Ndranghetism • Glocalism

In recent years, the mafia from Calabria has been at the centre of judicial interventions all around Italy and beyond. Usually known as the 'ndrangheta and, historically, also as the Honoured Society, the Calabrian mafia has been the object of media interest and scholarly work, at the point of redefining research and knowledge on (Italian) mafias more generally. Despite its only recent categorisation as a *mafia*, which, under Italian law, occurred only in 2010,[1] this mafia is as old as the Italian state and certainly as old as Sicilian Cosa Nostra, its most well-known relative. The debate on what constitutes a mafia, especially in the Italian context is still ongoing

© The Editor(s) (if applicable) and The Author(s) 2016   1
A. Sergi, A. Lavorgna, *'Ndrangheta*,
DOI 10.1007/978-3-319-32585-9_1

notwithstanding the longevity of the phenomenon and its literature. The term mafia indicates the prototypical case of criminal structures transcending class divisions and the divide between the illegal and legal (Von Lampe 2008). As argued by Italian scholars, mafia groups are those types of organised crime groups supported by social prestige and accepted and/ or tolerated by their own communities; they are also capable of infiltrating legal economy and politics (Sciarrone and Storti 2014; Sciarrone 2014). In particular, Sciarrone (2011) describes mafias as social forces with the power to accumulate and employ social capital; mafias are social structures realising *strategic* goals through different types of resources. These resources are the control of territory, affiliates, social relationships, and intimidation originating from the associative bond, money, and political power (Dalla Chiesa 2010). Individuals having access to such resources can be internal to the mafia group, or external in a populated "grey area" surrounding and strengthening mafia influence (Mete 2011; Ciconte 2013; Dalla Chiesa 2015). Within this framework, the 'ndrangheta is a mafia-type organisation with roots in Calabria, a region in the extreme south of Italy, at the "toe" of the peninsula but with clear projections and activities outside its birthplace.

The purpose of this book is twofold: first, it is an updated outlook on the various components that today support the attribution to the 'ndrangheta of the label of "most powerful Italian mafia" by authorities. This primacy is to be found in activities and roles of 'ndrangheta clans in various criminal markets in Italy and around the world. The second purpose of this work is to dig deeper in the concept of 'ndrangheta as a mafia-type organised crime group. This requires looking at the structure of the Calabrian clans, their organisational ties, and their movements abroad.

According to recent scholarly work the primacy of the 'ndrangheta can be linked to various elements: the 'ndrangheta is more reliable; it has substituted Cosa Nostra when the Sicilian mafia was at the centre of a political and media moral panic; it has a more flexible structure; and it is more present outside Calabria than other Italian mafias. Strategically, politically, financially, internationally, and culturally, the Calabrian mafia has been underestimated for a long time, while instead it was accumulating wealth and power and was settling outside of regional boundaries (Paoli 1994). This book wishes to critically unpack the claimed primacy of the 'ndrangheta among the Italian mafias by focusing on both the structures of the clans and on the criminal activities that ensure longevity and wealth to the affiliates and their networks.

The perspective under which we develop our analysis rejects the idea of "the 'ndrangheta" as a monolithic mafia organisation; we understand and explain the 'ndrangheta as a fragmented phenomenon, without, however, denying the existence of centralised coordination structures among the clans. We also promote a view of the 'ndrangheta as a *behavioural model*—a set of behaviours, which we could call *'ndranghetism*—rather than solely a set of criminal activities and organisational features (Sergi 2016a, 2016b). These behaviours are *qualifiers of a mafia behaviour* generally intended (i.e. applicable to other groups with similar characteristics, anywhere in the world), and appreciate mafias as social phenomena combining both cultural and structural elements.

This *behavioural model* encapsulates the ability to manipulate social networks and relationships, more or less linked to family dynamics and certainly entrenched in social structures—in this case, Calabrian ones; it is related to the manipulation of traditions, rituals, and social practices of communication and leadership among Calabrian individuals. This manipulation is secured through shared values and conducts, which do not necessarily amount to criminal conducts (such as family support, marriage among families to cement ties, and ways to behave in the community). The exploitation of shared values and social bonds—through the use of usurpation, arrogance, intimidation, violence, and subjugation—differentiates a *'ndranghetista* (affiliate of an 'ndrangheta clan) from the rest of the population. This phenomenon, which is cultural and social, can only prosper thanks to structural factors in society. Both structural weaknesses (such as a weak political class) and structural opportunities (such as the possibility to invest in new business ventures) allow *individuals subscribing and adopting the mafia behaviours* to prosper and further organise in more or less regulated groups with coordination functions as needed.

The successful intersection between cultural and structural elements forms what we name "mafia" also in accordance with the Italian Criminal Code. Article 416-*bis*, in fact, postulates the elements of the "mafia method" defined as the condition of subjugation, intimidation, and *omertà* that originate from the associative bonds existing among affiliates. Furthermore, the conceptualisation of "mafia" at the basis of article 416-*bis* is grounded in the sociological characteristics of the phenomenon: control of territory, interdependence among affiliates, potential use of violence, and organic relationships with politics (Dalla Chiesa 2010: 36). We argue, therefore, that rather than discussing the 'ndrangheta only as a criminal organisation—running the risk to eliminate subtle but necessary internal differences among the various manifestations of the phenomenon—it makes more sense to look at what the clans share in terms of their ability to exploit social values, relationships, and opportunities for the benefits of criminal activities. This exploitation occurs through a socially recognised *set of behaviours*, effective for a successful interaction with local communities, which are needed to disguise illegal activities, secure protection from prosecution, as well as to ensure social inclusion. This *behavioural model* becomes criminally relevant because prodromal to or even facilitating the use of violence, usurpation, and intimidation.

In brief this book considers the 'ndrangheta as a mafia-type *behaviour*, alongside its being a mafia-type *organisation*. On one side, judicial results have recently ascertained a unification of 'ndrangheta clans, under more or less hierarchical coordination structures in the southern part of Calabria, the hinterland of the capital city, Reggio Calabria. On the other side, the characteristics of this mafia and its links to the particular territory of Calabria contradict the idea of a full-blown total confederation in the whole region. Calabria is a highly fragmented region, culturally, geographically, and demographically. Some of these conditions date back to the unification of Italy and before, and are very visible to a keen eye visiting the area. Not only the distances, the roads, and the natural landscapes change significantly from one area of Calabria to the other, but also political settings, civil society's traits, and industrialisation processes are quite different across the region. Some of the most eminent historians in the area have often talked about many (plural) *Calabrie* (Cingari 1982; Sergi 1993).

Bearing in mind the plurality paradigm for an analysis of the Calabrian territory, we prefer to approach the 'ndrangheta as a *plural* and multifaceted phenomenon under the same collective name. Rather than the expansion of the 'ndrangheta as organisation growing in power, we observe a *'ndranghetisation* process across Calabria and beyond regional boundaries (Sergi 2016a). This process occurs also with the increasing use of the single word "'ndrangheta" applied as a brand name to indicate the mafia-type behaviour—*'ndranghetism*—of criminals and groups with a Calabrian connection. By *'ndranghetisation* we essentially indicate the process of imitation and osmosis among the clans in Calabria and outside the regional boundaries that allow us to identify similar *'ndranghetist* behaviours even when there are no signs of formal coordination structures in place among the clans across different territories. Certainly, the clans across the region share similar behaviours and, in the years, have increased their power and reach in various criminal markets, sign that the brand name works and their reputation is reinforced.

In practical terms, following this perspective means being careful about the language used throughout the book. For example, we tend not to use the singular name 'ndrangheta, but rather we refer to *'ndrangheta clans* or *'ndrine*. Whenever we do use the singular word, we usually refer to general mafia's presence and/or mafia's behaviours.

There have also been numerous debates and discussions on the name(s) of the 'ndrangheta in the first place. It is clear that the origins of the word are Greek (*andranghateia* means "society of men of honour", and *andrangathō* means "to engage in military actions")—which is more than plausible in the Calabrian territories that used to be part of the *Magna Graecia*. The use of the word 'ndrangheta to indicate a criminal phenomenon is also quite dated. As reported by linguistic scholars (Trumper et al. 2014) in the 1920s and 1930s, various documents from local police mention the terms *dranghita*, *entrangheta*, and similar others to indicate bullyism and subjugation from certain individuals across the region. However, one thing is the use of the term and the other is the attribution of meaning and the evolution of a concept around that term. The latter needs to be found in Calabrian history rather than in linguistics.

Starting from these conceptualisations and clarifications of our position, this book presents the 'ndrangheta, as both mafia-type organisation and a mafia-type behavioural model, deeply linked to Calabria and its fragmentation, and highly present outside the local birthplace. Hence, the *glocal* adjective we chose for the title (Hobbs 1998).

We have organised the book in two parts. The first part, Part I, will describe the evolution of the 'ndrangheta as a social phenomenon in Calabria and the movement of the clans in the rest of Italy and abroad. It will look at the birth of the 'ndrangheta as social drive of Calabria and particularly at the way the clans gained and still retain an important role within Calabrian economy. Also, this part will specifically consider the migration of the clans and their activities abroad, within paradigms of colonisation and delocalisation, settlement and outsourcing of activities, by critically linking migration of Calabrian individuals and families to the exportation of criminal savoir faire to the rest of Italy and beyond. Part II will look more specifically at the criminal activities of the clans, with a specific focus on the roles of the Calabrian *'ndrine* in the transnational dimension of the drug trade and money laundering, and with further focus on their investments and interferences with waste disposal, the green economy, the food industry, and even online gambling. The choice of the two parts is in alignment with Block's famous understanding of New York's criminal organisations as power and enterprise syndicates (Block 1980). Using Block's (1980: 129) conceptualisation, we can describe the 'ndrangheta both as power syndicate—retaining control over the territory—and as enterprise syndicate, as the clans are successful in pursuing a number of illegal activities, both locally and nationally or internationally (Asmundo 2011; Paoli 2003; Ruggiero 1996; Sergi 2015). We argue that the 'ndrangheta is a poly-crime mafia and that the clans originate their strength and increase their criminal reach thanks to well-balanced investments into both power and enterprise capacities (Busso and Storti 2011); they are both sociopolitical actors and successful criminal entrepreneurs (Sciarrone 2011).

Our analysis is based on the judicial work of offices of the District Antimafia Directorates (DDA). As qualitative social scientists, we do not wish to simply take the words of law enforcement as indisputable truth; indeed, when actually looking at the judicial documents of the various operations—including interceptions and witnesses' declarations—the picture is complex and in need of interpretation. In order to understand the evolution and the growth of the 'ndrangheta, it is necessary to remember that it is also thanks to the *static* elements of the region—as we will see, its geographical fragmentation, its political weaknesses, and its economic underdevelopment—that the clans have developed into the *dynamic* forces that they are today. Finally, the book's twofold focus, on structures and activities, reflects our underlying conceptualisation of the 'ndrangheta as a set of behaviours (*'ndranghetism*) spreading thanks to a *'ndranghetisation* process as previously defined.

Before leaving the readers to the rest of the book, it is necessary to present a map of the Calabrian region, which should serve as a reference for the geographical mentions made throughout the book (Fig. 1.1).

In this map, the dividing lines highlight the main areas of interest for our analysis. South, opposite of Sicily, is Reggio Calabria, capital of the region and very contested area for the birth, the evolution, and the coordination of many 'ndrangheta clans. Above the city of Reggio is the Aspromonte mountain, a protected natural area near San Luca, which, in the years, has assumed crucial importance geographically and symbolically for the clans: the Aspromonte divides the clans in the east of the city of Reggio Calabria from those in the west of the city. Generally speaking, any reference to the 'ndrangheta as a monolithic criminal organisation de facto refers to the organisation of those clans in the area around Reggio Calabria, in the map.

Fig. 1.1 Map of Calabria. Source of map: d-maps.com

In the middle of the region, around the city of Vibo Valentia, is the area of the port of Gioia Tauro, crucial for the drug trade, as we will see. Clans from the areas of Catanzaro, Crotone, and Cosenza are usually referred to as more chaotic and less organised than those of Reggio Calabria, but their expansion beyond the regional boundaries often confirms their reach into criminal markets as well as their changing organisational structure.

NOTE

1. With the word "'ndrangheta" added to the offence of mafia membership in article 416-*bis* of the Italian Criminal Code (law decree converted with changes from Law No. 50, 31 March 2010, in *Gazzetta Ufficiale* 03.04.2010, No.78).

REFERENCES

Asmundo A. (2011). Indicatori e costi della criminalita' mafiosa. In: R. Sciarrone (ed) *Alleanze nell'Ombra: Mafie ed economie locali in Sicilia e nel Mezzogiorno.* Roma: Donzelli.

Block, A. (1980). *East Side—West Side. Organizing Crime in New York 1930–1950,* Cardiff: University College Cardiff Press.

Busso, S., and Storti, L. (2011). I contesti di alta densita' mafiosa: un quadro socio-economico. In: R. Sciarrone (ed) *Alleanze nell'Ombra: Mafie ed economie locali in Sicilia e nel Mezzogiorno.* Roma: Donzelli.

Ciconte, E. (2013). *Politici (e) malandrini.* Soveria Mannelli: Rubbettino.

Cingari, G. (1982). *Storia della Calabria dall'Unità a Oggi.* Bari: Editori Laterza.

Dalla Chiesa, N. (2010). *La convergenza. Mafia e politica nella Seconda Repubblica.* Melampo: Milano.

Dalla Chiesa, N. (2015). A proposito di Mafia Capitale. Alcuni Problemi Teorici. *CROSS. Rivista di Studi e Ricerche sulla Criminalità Organizzata,* 1(2): DOI: 10.13130/cross-16634.

Hobbs, D. (1998). Going Down the Glocal: The Local Context of Organised Crime. *The Howard Journal of Criminal Justice,* 37(4), 407–422.

Mete, V. (2011). Scioglimenti, dati in rete contro il silenzio. *Guida agli Enti Locali.* Il Sole 24 Ore.

Paoli, L. (1994). An underestimated criminal phenomenon: the Calabrian 'Ndrangheta. *European Journal of Crime, Criminal Law and Criminal Justice,* 3, 212–238.

Paoli, L. (2003). *Mafia brotherhoods: Organized crime, Italian style.* Oxford, New York: Oxford University Press.

Ruggiero, V. (1996). *Organized and corporate crime in Europe : Offers that can't be refused.* Aldershot: Dartmouth.

Sciarrone, R. (2011). Mafie, relazioni e affari nell'area grigia. In: R. Sciarrone (ed) *Alleanze nell'ombra. Mafie ed economie locali in Sicilia e nel Mezzogiorno.* Roma: Donzelli.

Sciarrone, R. (2014). Tra sud e nord. Le mafie nelle aree non tradizionali. In: R. Sciarrone (ed.), *Mafie al Nord. Strategie criminali e contesti locali.* Rome: Donzelli Editore.

Sciarrone, R., & Storti, L. (2014). The territorial expansion of mafia-type organized crime. The case of the Italian mafia in Germany. *Crime, Law and Social Change, 61*(1), 37–60.

Sergi, P. (1993). *Le Mie Calabrie.* Soveria Mannelli: Rubbettino.

Sergi, A. (2015). Mafia and politics as concurrent governance actors. Revisiting political power and crime in Southern Italy. In P. C. Van Duyne, A. Maljević, G. A. Antonopoulos, et al. (Eds.), *The relativity of wrongdoing: Corruption, organised crime, fraud and money laundering in perspective.* Oisterwijk: Wolf Legal Publishers.

Sergi, A. (2016a). Meet the Ndrangheta – and why it's time to bust some myths about the Calabrian mafia, The Conversation, 4 February 2016, https://the-conversation.com/meet-the-ndrangheta-and-why-its-time-to-bust-some-myths-about-the-calabrian-mafia-54075

Sergi, A. (2016b). 'Countering the Australian 'Ndrangheta. The criminalisation of mafia behaviour in Australia between national and comparative criminal law'. Australian and New Zealand Journal of Criminology (in press)

Trumper, J. b., Maddalon, M., Nicaso, A., et al. (2014). *Male Lingue Vecchi e Nuovi Codici delle Mafie.* Cosenza: Pellegrini.

Von Lampe, K. (2008). Organized crime in Europe: conceptions and realities Policing. *A Journal of Policy and Practice, 2*(1), 7–17.

PART I

Structures and Governance

CHAPTER 2

Calabria and the 'Ndrangheta

Abstract As qualified minority of Calabrian society, the 'ndrangheta is today a mafia-type criminal system, supported by social prestige and embedded in society. As any other mafia, the clans of the 'ndrangheta have growth in parallel to the evolution of their region. This chapter will look at the historical evolution of the clans and their relationships with the rest of the Calabrian society. The 'ndrangheta clans share characteristics of other mafia-type organised crime groups whose power is enforced through violence and through the exploitation of cultural codes and social relationships in Calabria.

Keywords Calabria • Southern Italy • Underdevelopment • Mafia Evolution • Mafia–Politics Nexus

INTRODUCTION

Summarising the origins and the growth of the 'ndrangheta clans in Calabria, also known as *'ndrine*, is very complex. Firstly, we cannot separate the birth and development of the mafia phenomenon from the historical evolution of Calabria. Secondly, the identification of sociological factors, which, in Calabria, have contributed to the contemporary situation of the clans, is, in retrospective, not an easy task. While, on the one hand, the Calabrian region is an example of underdevelopment in Italy,

© The Editor(s) (if applicable) and The Author(s) 2016   13
A. Sergi, A. Lavorgna, *'Ndrangheta*,
DOI 10.1007/978-3-319-32585-9_2

on the other hand, the clans have prospered also thanks to the changes of Calabrian society, both financial and political. What we call 'ndrangheta, the Calabrian mafia, exhibits the traits of any mafia-type organisation and some structural peculiarities linked to the territory (Sciarrone 2009). This chapter will select some events in Calabrian history, to identify how and why the evolution of the mafia clans is symbiotically linked to Calabrian society. For the 'ndrangheta clans everything starts where it ends, in Calabria. An investigation of the complex and composite identity of the clans in their birthplace is essential to fully see the various faces of this mafia today, also outside Calabria.

HISTORICAL BACKGROUND OF THE EVOLUTION OF THE 'NDRANGHETA IN CALABRIA

Corrado Alvaro, an Italian writer born in San Luca, in the Aspromonte mountain, wrote in an article in the national newspaper *Il Corriere della Sera* on the 17 September 1955 (Cingari 1982: 367):

> The Fibbia, the 'ndrina, the 'ndranghita, the Honoured Society, basically the mafia, I have known since I can remember. In my meetings in Calabria, I have always been interested in noticing those attitudes, those behaviours, those particular hairstyles or clothes that might characterise a member of the Honoured Society. Far from assuming brutal appearances, they acted like distinguished *parvenu*. Strong through violence, they had social status. Despised in the past, they became feared. When a society has very few or no occasions to change its *status quo*, to be feared is a way to emerge. This is not a simple policing issue; it is not even useful to blame the whole province. The norm for a serious action could be found through an exam of how the governing class has acted in the past 50 years. This is not all, but it is a starting point.

Even though these affirmations date back to 1955, they still are quite relevant today. Indeed, the evolution of the clans and their affiliates, their behaviours within and outside Calabria and specifically certain areas of Calabria, is tightly linked to the destiny endured by the region as a whole, in its political, financial, and social settings.

The origins of what today we call 'ndrangheta are legendary and linked to the myth of three Spanish knights—Osso, Mastrosso, and Carcagnosso—who funded the Honoured Society in the fifteenth century, together with the other Italian mafias, on the model of the "Honoured Society of the Garduna in Toledo" (Ciconte 2011; Sergi 1991; Casaburi

2010). The birth of the Calabrian mafia is usually placed before or during the unification of Italy in 1861. It is not only a Calabrian discourse that links the phenomenon of mafia with the dissolution of the feudal system but also the introduction of capitalism in the rural areas of the south of Italy. Calabrian anthropologist Lombardi Satriani has been among the firsts to discuss the link between capitalism, underdevelopment, and mafias. More specifically, Lombardi Satriani maintains that the "peculiar socio-historical concretisation, which we call mafia" is a product of a "dependent capitalism" that the Italian State has fostered in the south of Italy, and especially in Calabria since the unification of Italy. This is paired with the absence of other private forms of entrepreneurship and with the presence of a subculture based on certain family and social values (Pitaro 1996: 50).

Until 1960s, historians and journalists (Cingari 1982; Malafarina 1981a) describe clans, especially in the Aspromonte mountain near Reggio Calabria, as a mix of bandits and aggregations of "men of honour". The Chief of Police Marzano was sent by the Ministry of Interior to eradicate the mafia from the territory in the mid-1950s (Malafarina 1981b), showing that the problem was already known, even though not fully understood. Since the 1960s, however, there have been a number of events that have profoundly affected the Calabrian region and also its mafia clans. If we had to choose among the relevant factors that in the history of Calabria have been significant for the evolution of the 'ndrangheta clans we need to highlight the following:

- The extensive migration from the region, especially in the aftermath of the Second World War;
- The political turmoil surrounding the birth of the regional entity;
- The failures of industrialisation in the region.

As for the first point, the next two chapters of this book will specifically deal with the relationships between 'ndrangheta clans and Calabrian migration. In general, the ability of the clans to exploit the links with Calabrian migrants settled outside the region has been facilitated and strengthened by the very tight family bonds forming Calabrian society, as also described later in this chapter.

As for the second point, the events surrounding the establishment of the Calabrian region as a state entity in 1970 had created different types of political tensions in the region, which culminated between July 1970 and

February 1971 in the so-called Moti di Reggio, riots in Reggio Calabria. The riots eventually ended, after the involvement of the army, when it was decided for the city of Catanzaro to be the executive capital city and Reggio Calabria to be the administrative one: this fragmentation of political power still characterises the region. Behind the riots in Reggio were very deep social problems linked to the area around the city (D'Agostini 1972), such as the profound divide between demographic dimensions and fragility of production activities, the frustration for the general situation and the lack of identity of the city of Reggio due to its vicinity to Sicily, and the perceived distance from other areas of Calabria (Cingari 1982; Ciconte 1992). In those years, all the difficulties of a city that kept enlarging but was struggling to grow in terms of services and opportunities made social exclusion even more a characteristic of the extreme south of the region.

This is obviously linked to the third point, the failure of a process of industrialisation, always promised and never realised. There are a few too many examples of failed projects in Calabria between the 1960s and the 1980s. Probably the most well known is the "Pacchetto Colombo", a series of investment plans which were meant to boost the economy of the region (Coscarelli 1992). Among these plans were the expansion of the motorway A3 started in 1964 between the neighbouring regions Campania and Basilicata, connecting Salerno (in the Campania region) and Reggio Calabria, and the construction of the port of Gioia Tauro. The port was only finished at the beginning of the 1990s, while the Salerno–Reggio motorway in 2016 is still awaiting completion, becoming one of the most shameful delays in Italian economy (Sergi and South 2016). Other plans—mainly linked to chemical, iron, and steel industrial centres—failed miserably too; today their ruins look like an industrial graveyard of desolation across the region.

Calabria has always swung between potential for development and underdevelopment. Since the Second World War, it has represented "*the negative paradigm of the inhomogeneous development of the country*" (Sergi 2013: 136). On one side the potential for development, when accompanied by injections of public funds, has been hijacked by a network of well-connected families, tied by blood and by favour exchanges. On the other side, underdevelopment and the stagnation of economy—due to difficult political choices in the tremendously fractured realities of the region—fed into the preservation of a mafia-type social structure, which praises usurpation and violence for social and economic promotion.

CAPITAL ACCUMULATION BETWEEN VIOLENCE AND ENTREPRENEURSHIP

Some of the considerations made in the previous paragraphs already give us an idea of the extremely complex scenario in which the mafia prospered in Calabria. Certainly, when entering the classic debate in organised crime studies between culturalism and structuralism, Calabria represents a challenging case for both perspectives. It fits both. On one side, the 'ndrangheta is entrenched in its culture. It is undoubtedly Calabrian. This does not mean that it is *only* Calabrian, but the way members of the 'ndrangheta behave among each others, the value of the family bonds, the importance of social prestige in small villages of Calabria, the words they are caught using in the interceptions, the rural geography, and the scars of a very complex past are also culturally relevant indicators of Calabrian society (Teti 2015). However, if the cultural elements might have supported the preservation, they do not explain neither the birth nor the evolution of the 'ndrangheta as a criminal behaviour. These are rooted in the structural weaknesses of Calabrian economy and politics (Paoli 2003). As maintained by Granovetter (1973: 1377) when looking at ties in social networks, *"the personal experience of individuals is closely bound up with larger-scale aspects of social structure"*; it would be impossible to understand how the clans work at the micro level without looking at the macro level they are embedded in.

Within the socio-economic scenario briefly described above, we need to investigate the way mafia power grew. How did the 'ndrangheta—as a mafia organisation and subsequently as *a behavioural model* and *brand*— evolve in a territory like the Calabrian region at the dawn of the 1900? The answer lies in the accumulation of money and in an increasing ability to govern the territory of certain families and individuals later organised in small criminal structures. The financial wealth of the clans came from both legal and illegal sources in the form of a preliminary capital accumulation (Dalla Chiesa 2010). First, men affiliated to 'ndrangheta clans operated a strategic infiltration and participation in the entrepreneurial soul of the region since the 1970s; second, impressive amount of money was stored during the kidnapping season throughout the 1980s.

As seen above, the injection of public funds in Calabria since the 1970s has been an occasion for the clans to infiltrate the economy while building on their public profiles. Antimafia investigations have proved mafia infiltration in public funds and projects as important as the port of Gioia

Tauro and the A3 Salerno–Reggio Calabria motorway (Mete 2011a). Specifically, but not only, Operation Porto[1] and Operation Arca[2] have demonstrated how the clans had created a consortium to buy out contractors and subcontractors in the building of the port and the motorway. We read in Operation Arca[3] about a proper *system*:

> The agreement among the clans and between the clans and the contractors (usually a company outside Calabria) had already been established before the work started by planning operational directives. Each clan had control of the portion of motorway in its own territory, supervised by the stronger clans in Reggio city.

Operation Arca also described how the clans controlled their "portions" in a number of ways: first, through fictitious ownership of assets and use of frontmen to guarantee access to payments, to manage subcontracts by twisting prices and discourage competition, to inflate costs to mask extortion rackets (an "environmental tax", around 3 %), and to hire workers. Second, the clans used intimidation and violence to dissuade any competitor left or resisting.

A very similar scenario is the one described in the interceptions for Operation Porto. Mr Bianchi, a man close to the federation of clans in Gioia Tauro, says to Mr Walter Lugli, entrepreneur in a company working in the port, in Milan on 16 September 1996[4]:

> We are by your side, for any problem you have down there we can be by your side in any way, any problem you might have or you are going to have, with any possible means. Naturally, and I think it's only fair, you know with all that hectares of land, the gardens cut off, the cultivations of oranges and mandarins destroyed, I think it's only fair that we get something too. Our request is… it's not about hiring someone or similar things, it's about creating, later maybe, something… some activity nearby, through you, and our request now is a contribution for what you do there.

The mafia *behaviour* is evident and it is about controlling the territory, both financially and through military/violent control of the territory ("with any possible means"). Mr Bianchi continues by explaining its seemingly legal request:

> We are there, we live there, we own the past, the present, the future. Our request is that for every container of yours there is something for us, we

consider that logic, fair. It's an exchange, it's reciprocal, correct, so... our request is a dollar and a half for every container you disembark, it's nothing.[5]

Through semi-legal activities, 'ndrangheta families secured impressive amounts of money, usually invested in more profitable activities such as cigarette smuggling or drugs later on. Another source of their wealth has been the numerous kidnappings. The first kidnappings in Calabria date back to the 1950s, and it is in 1973 that Paul Getty III was abducted in Rome by 'ndrangheta affiliates in the first case of this kind that reached national media (Sergi 1991). The "kidnapping season"—the serial use of abduction for ransom—is one of the nastiest pages of regional history, and it is also the period that gave the 'ndrangheta visibility in Italy and among the other unaware and honest citizens of Calabria, who often spoke out to support the families of those kidnapped. The kidnapping season refers to a period that goes from mid-1970s to the beginning of the 1990s and counted for more than 200 kidnappings all across Italy, especially in Lombardia and in Calabria, by groups more or less linked to 'ndrangheta clans in the Aspromonte where the abducted people were also kept (Casaburi 2010; Ciconte 2011). The numbers are not specific because at that time other criminal organisations in Italy were also engaging in the same practice and there is uncertainty in the attribution of some kidnappings (Sergi 1991). Estimates of that period count proceeds between 250 and 400 billion Italian liras (about 270–430 million euros today) (Fontana and Serarcangeli 1991; Ciconte 2011). According to the Antimafia Parliamentary Commission, this money was invested in cigarette smuggling during the 1970s and 1980s and in drugs in the 1980s and 1990s in a Marxist logic of capital accumulation; also, part of the money was laundered abroad, especially in Germany and Australia (Forgione 2008; Macrì and Ciconte 2009).

Scholars have talked about a transition between an *old mafia*, very local, archaic, and brutally involved in the kidnappings, and a *new* one, the *entrepreneurial* mafia, capitalising through drugs and infiltration in the legal economy (Arlacchi 1986). While obviously being a social construction, this transition between an old face and the modern one has been anything but smooth. Between the 1970s and the 1990s, in fact, escalations of violence have stained villages and cities of Calabria with bloodshed of mafia feuds. The feuds are the visible face of the fight for military supremacy of mafia clans on their territories. In the area around Reggio Calabria for example, between 1974 and 1977, a feud caused over 200 victims across various clans; between 1985 and 1991 another feud caused over 700 victims (Ciconte 2011). They broadly related to the control over both territories and illicit markets and to disagreement in the strategy and the management of the clans.

All feuds profoundly changed alliances in every area of Calabria. The mafia war in the 1970s caused a generational change in the clans near Reggio. The new generation, while still fighting for the control of cigarette smuggling and drugs routes, also understood the need (and fetched the possibility) to interact with higher powers in the region, namely masonic lodges and political class, as we will see later in this chapter. Upon ceasing the hostilities of another mafia war in the 1980s, the clans reached the so-called *pax mafiosa* also thanks to the intervention of clans of Sicilian Cosa Nostra (Ciconte 2011; Casaburi 2010). By 1991, the structure and organisation of the Calabrian clans appeared drastically changed with new alliances and the recognition of coordination structures especially in the area of Reggio Calabria, the one with the highest density of families. This has been explained in Operation Olimpia,[6] which has been the first and one of the most important investigations in the structure of the clans at the beginning of the 1990s. It was the dawn of the 1990s and the 'ndrangheta had started showing its contemporary traits, where both faces of the clans—the old and the new, the power-hungry and the entrepreneurial souls—co-exist in constantly developing forms, with the city of Reggio Calabria at the centre of Antimafia focus.

POLITICS, MASONIC ALLIANCES, AND CONCURRENT GOVERNANCE

Control of the territory does not only mean violence, truces, and alliances; it also means political interests and power over the *res publica*. In 1994, in their request for preventative measures to the judge for preliminary investigations during Operation Olimpia,[7] the District Antimafia Directorates (DDA) of Reggio Calabria wrote that in the past decades there had been:

> [...] a radical mutation in the "culture" and in the politics of the 'ndrangheta. Such mutation goes from an attitude of antagonism, or at least detachment, from civil society, to an attitude of integration, in order to search for new forms of legitimation, not limited to criminal powers, but extended to politics, economics and the institutions.

The relationships between mafia and politics and mafia and masonic lodges are in Calabria much more fluid than just corruption pacts and/ or infiltration in public or private affairs. Antimafia prosecutors in Reggio Calabria do not hesitate to say that "*the 'ndrangheta is politics*" and that "*it is all about masonry*",[8] as the clans live together with—they often are— elite powers in the region. Again, when we look at the socio-economic history of the region, this does not surprise (Cavaliere 2004). It does not surprise in general to find alliances with politics, as this is typical behaviour of every mafia: political proximity, social power, and influence are the distinguishing factor of mafia groups. Indeed, as noticed by Catanzaro (1992: 43), mafias' main network systems are sustained by three types of relations: kinship, patronage, and friendship. These factors are the ingredients for a successful control of the territory through social consensus.

This is perfectly visible, for example, also in the use of religion as reinforcement of the social presence and consensus of the clans, typical, again, of every mafia group (Sales 2010; Dino 2008). Moreover, to support the legitimacy of the clans to appear in religious parades and to participate in the spiritual life of their villages, 'ndrangheta men can count on a whole set of religious references in the various rituals of affiliation (Ciconte 2015) and in the symbols of the 'ndrangheta codes (Trumper et al. 2014) meant to promote the mafia's collective "narcissism" (Di Forti 1982).

The spectrum of illegality is further complicated by the perspective that sees mafia and politicians having relationships for mutual benefits (Çayli 2010), which eventually might become a form of "*concurrent governance*" (Sergi 2015: 43) between the two, with manipulation of elections, exchanges of favours for votes, and shared interests. In case of dissent, the clans have not hesitated to display their antagonism to the political class. The murder of Francesco Fortugno, Vice-President of the Regional Council of Calabria, on 16 October 2005, which happened in Locri (East coast in the province of Reggio Calabria) in full day light and in public during election day, was a clear affirmation of power and *hubris* by the clans (Forgione 2008).

Since the 1970s, if not before—while mafia clans were investing in legal economy, surviving feuds, and pursuing more ambitious illegal activities such as cigarette smuggling and drug trade—the relationship with political and social elites was part of the transformation process. In continuity with the previous decades, especially since the aftermath of the Second World War, Calabrian political classes in the 1970s were at the mercy of personal interests of a closed elite (Cingari 1982). Operation Olimpia has also analysed the relationships with politics and masonic lodges since the 1970s. Specifically, in one of the sentences of the appeal trial of Olimpia[9] the judges say:

> Our witness [...] knew of a "commission" due to administer all the illicit interests of the city of Reggio Calabria; this commission had been created after the *pax mafiosa*, in 1992–1993, by mafia members, politicians, masons, and entrepreneurs.

The links between mafia and politics in Calabria have been cemented through the links with masonic lodges, historically intersecting with certain political elites (Cordova 2014). These connections meant contact with those social classes usually members of masonic lodges: professionals, entrepreneurs, members of law enforcement, and also politicians. Obviously these contacts have proved useful to cover up and facilitate new investments in the legal economy as well as for protection from the criminal justice system to the point that the clans became *"invisible"* for the authorities (Forgione 2008: 32).

Antimafia operations of the 1990s have clarified that only a certain type of 'ndrangheta members could access the exclusive and reserved masonic lodges: a new managerial and elite rank in the 'ndrangheta, the *Santa*, granted only to few bosses, became the *trait-d'union* between mafia, masonry, and obviously politics (Sergi 1991; Ciconte 2013; Guarino 2004). Even today, as confirmed by a number of operations, such as All Inside II[10] and Crimine,[11] the *Santa* represents the highest ranking of affiliation. The various codes of rituals contain formulas for the attribution of the *Santa*, together with other rankings (Ciconte 2015; Nicaso and Gratteri 2012). In Operation All Inside II, letters and interceptions of 'ndrangheta members reveal the way the ranking (known as "the flower", *il fiore*, or "the gift", *la dote*) of the *Santa* is conferred to those who deserve it, in secret, by those who already have it: *"I am happy for the 'flower' that you received; you know very few have it here in Platì and only who has it can know about it."*[12] In Operation Bellu Lavuru,[13] the reference to two groups of people, one *visible* and one *invisible*, confirms the existence of a circle of 'ndrangheta affiliates close to the masonic lodges and to politics. In Operation Crimine,[14] which is the investigation that proved the existence of a unitary structure for the clans in the area of Reggio Calabria, the Antimafia prosecutors present a picture of the city of Reggio Calabria in the first decade of 2000s with very concerning degrees of infiltration in the legal sectors and in politics. Operation Reale[15] confirmed the presence of the clans in Reggio Calabria operating even within the university in the city of Reggio through political ties. In 2012, after months of work to establish the extent of mafia infiltration in the public administration of Reggio Calabria, an Investigative Commission (Commissione di Accesso 2012: 4) concluded:

> During the months of work this Commission has found that, in many aspects of the administrative life of the Council of Reggio Calabria, there are grave irregularities, inefficiencies and incongruences, gross negligence, actions and misbehaviours, which certainly have made the Council more easily permeable to the interests of the local mafia clans.

This brought to the dissolution[16] of the city council of Reggio Calabria in accordance with law decree 164/1991 (Mete 2013): Reggio Calabria's council was seen to be run in concurrent governance by politicians and mafia clans mutually benefitting from each other and linked by elite ties. There have been other ten city councils in Calabria dissolved for mafia infiltration in 2012, but certainly the events of Reggio Calabria have raised major concerns (Sergi 2015). The city of Reggio seems to be at the centre of every speculation of shadiness in Calabria, at the centre of the escalation of power of the clans, at the centre of dangerous relationships among mafia, politics, masonry, secret services, and finance (Prestifilippo 1998). Journalists, scholars, and magistrates in the past couple of decades have incessantly written and warned about the mafia–politics–masonry nexus in Calabria, painting a depressing picture of a region and in particular of a city, Reggio Calabria, ruled by *"a set of opportunities and ties that bond the various actors and form networks of collusion, not necessarily starting from mafia interests"* (Mete 2011b: 336).

'NDRANGHETA AND *'NDRANGHETE* TODAY

Those who are familiar with the social and economic history of Calabria know the paradigm of *le Calabrie* (plural), which encapsulates the idea of a divided region, geographically fractured, polycentric, and whose provinces often experience different speeds of development and different outcomes in evolution (Violante 1994; Sergi 1993; Cingari 1982). Indeed, the socio-economic history of the region confirms this fractured reality. As anticipated in the introduction to this book, in the various *Calabrie* we find different '*ndranghete* (plural); the mafia phenomenon in Calabria is plural. It is necessary to differentiate the characteristics of the 'ndrangheta behaviour in the different parts of the region. This differentiation is often overlooked and creates confusion when attempting to study the 'ndrangheta outside its regional boundaries. By looking at the different '*ndranghete* on the territory today, we can fully see the complexity of the phenomenon, its peculiarities, and its constant swinging between tradition and modernity. To facilitate the analysis we can divide the territorial analysis of the 'ndrangheta as follows:

- The province and the city of Reggio Calabria, especially the area of the Aspromonte region (the south of Calabria);
- The area of Vibo Valentia, Lamezia Terme, and Catanzaro (the centre of Calabria);
- The area of Crotone and Cosenza (the north and north-East of Calabria).

The province of Reggio Calabria, more than the others, represents the continuity between the mafia from the mountains (the Aspromonte) of the 1940s and the 1950s and the mafia of the cities, linked to politics and finance. It is not useful to differentiate between new and old mafia, as in Calabria the clans have evolved without interruptions and are still evolving every day. It can however be said, as argued by an Antimafia prosecutor in Reggio, that the clans in the area of Reggio Calabria *"have a very old heart and a very modern soul"*.[17] Prosecutors have tried for two decades to prove that the 'ndrangheta in Reggio has a vertex structure and they have finally succeeded in Operation Crimine.[18] While it has always been clear that the clans operated in alliance with each other, in consortia, and in federations of families, Operation Crimine judicially proved for the first time in 2012 that the 'ndrangheta in Reggio Calabria is united and that it is made of three *mandamenti* (subsections): the "Tirrenian" (the West coast of the province of Reggio), the "Ionic" (the East coast of the province of Reggio), and the "Centre" (the city of Reggio), with other middle units in between, all under the guidance of a collegial structure called *Crimine* or *Provincia*. This structure is not new and in the years has changed many names, including the *Santa*, or *il Padrino* (the Godfather).[19] This is essentially a structure of coordination of the various clans in the province of Reggio and their (individual or collective) projections in the north of Italy and abroad. Operation Crimine has showed that there is equilibrium between the centralisation of directives among the clans and their autonomy in business. It is not a hierarchical structure, rather a consortium of clans that are equal in autonomy and that "elect" a collegial central structure in case disagreements arise. It is this structure that today we can call "the 'ndrangheta".

Furthermore, it is in the province of Reggio that we find the oldest mafia families with the strongest reputation. Girolamo Molé, of the Molé clan in Gioia Tauro, intercepted on 27 September 2007 during Operation Cento Anni di Storia[20] ("100 Years of History"), is caught saying to his nephew:

> Here, we have 100 years of history... you cannot ruin that! If you want to create an alliance or you want to stay on your own, there is a way to do things right, you have to know that history counts, sacrifices, prison and everything else, everything counts, we respect the past and we respect history and we will never be wrong!

There is indeed a way to do things right. The first level of association among the clans is called *locale*. As the *'ndrina* is family based, it is not always linked to a specific territory; the *locale* groups the families with influence in a given municipality and with links outside Calabria. Ulterior groupings are the *minor* and *major societies*, formed according to family ties also beyond the boundaries of certain territories, clans' relevance on the territory, and the ranking given to clans' affiliates (the "minor" is the group of the lower-level affiliates and the "major" is made of the higher-ranking ones). This organisational structure is quite similar across the entire region, but it remains fluid and with some differences in other provinces. The essential peculiarity of the structure is indeed that the clans are based on *families* and not on territories, as it was for Sicilian Cosa Nostra (Pignatone and Prestipino 2013). This means that family and blood relationships can eventually bring an affiliate to belong to a *locale* distant from its birthplace; similarly, the *'ndrine* and the *locali* are recognisable through their family trees and family *surnames* rather than by their location. As clearly explained in the words of an Antimafia prosecutor in Reggio[21]:

> It is beyond confirmed that we have unity among the clans in the province of Reggio. You have Reggio city and its four main *'ndrine* that run extortion rackets together. You have Gioia Tauro and the port—Gioia Tauro is not only the port by the way—and then you have the Aspromonte, the villages of San Luca, Platì, historical families and alliances. There is such a diversity

[...] and every *locale* might have their own business here or elsewhere, but they all recognise the *Crimine*, they all know what others are doing and how to keep the peace and benefit from it.

Fundamental in the geography of clans in the province of Reggio are the *'ndrine* from the Aspromonte, from villages like San Luca, Platì, Sinopoli, and Africo. For the religious importance of the Madonna di Polsi—the so-called Madonna of the Mountain—in the rituals and in the symbolism of the 'ndrangheta (Trumper et al. 2014; Ciconte 2015), the villages in the Aspromonte receive a different type of treatment, they are respected, they represent the memory of the past, and the continuation in the present of the strength of family bonds throughout the last few decades. It is not by chance that the *Crimine* in Reggio is also known as the *Crimine di Polsi* (DNA 2011) and that a monetary contribution has to be paid by the affiliates to the *"Mamma di San Luca"* also outside Calabria.[22] The clans of the Aspromonte keep their position of supremacy in the formation of new *locali* and in the agreement of promotions and rankings as Operation Crimine confirmed during police raids at the festivities for the Madonna di Polsi[23] (end of August, beginning of September, each year) (DNA 2011). However, they might not keep their leverage outside the province of Reggio Calabria, in other areas of the region where the 'ndrangheta appears quite diverse.

The element of diversity among the clans is a constant of the Calabrian mafia phenomenon. In the area of Vibo Valentia and Catanzaro, geographically adjacent to the province of Reggio Calabria, the clans engage in different types of activities, both locally and outside Calabria; they are often structured differently from those in Reggio and are not under the *Crimine*. The DDA in Catanzaro, which has jurisdiction over the provinces of Catanzaro, Vibo Valentia, Crotone, and Cosenza, necessarily assesses changes and alliances between the clans in their areas and the ones in the area of Reggio. One of the chief prosecutors in Catanzaro[24] specifies:

> The destiny of the clans in Vibo and Catanzaro is necessarily bound to the clans of Gioia Tauro and generally the Reggio area. Geographically, the port is in between the two provinces, Reggio and Vibo, therefore alliances to import drugs and coordination over the territory are everyday's business.

According to the National Antimafia Directorate (DNA 2015) the *'ndrine* in the Catanzaro district (mainly Vibo and Catanzaro and the city of Lamezia Terme) are often not as stable as the ones in Reggio: there are, for example, ongoing feuds related to the allocation of construction contracts and subcontracts (mainly for touristic resorts and their supply of food). Even though it cannot be said that there exist in the area a chamber of control or coordination structure, some of the clans (like the *'ndrina* Mancuso or the *'ndrina* Pesce) have a solid reputation, especially in relation to the port of Gioia Tauro and the drug trade, and conspicuous wealth that allow them to unofficially become the main criminal entities of the area. Also, they have been cultivating tight links with politics, which allow them to exercise considerable political pressure (Senato della Repubblica 2015).

Moreover, specifically for the area of Crotone and to a lesser extent Cosenza, as an Antimafia prosecutor in Catanzaro reveals:

> In operation Kyterion, in 2015, we have seen something different. First of all, there is a condition of parity among the clans, and most of all, equality among the clans in the area of Crotone, the East coast of the province of Cosenza, and those in the Ionic part of Reggio Calabria. Second, we know that the person who we believe was the highest in ranking (now in jail) wanted to create also in his area (everything but Vibo Valentia which remained under the control of Reggio) a similar structure to the *Crimine* in Reggio. The idea of unifying the clans more formally now runs also in Crotone, but as something different from the Reggio's one.   ·

This is a clear example of *'ndranghetisation*, where some of the clans in the north-east of the region are willing or attempting to imitate the structure of those in Reggio Calabria, through the same behaviours (DNA 2016). The geography of the clans in today's Calabria operates in a condition of continuity and similarity across the region. However, there is a clear difference between the clans in Reggio Calabria and the ones in the rest of the region. This difference is neither in the basic organisational structure—still unitary and based on the clans and their alliances—nor is in their power, their wealth, their links with others outside Calabria, nor in their behaviour on the territory. The clans in Reggio appear *denser* and more advanced in their unification. As Pino Neri—a lawyer and a 'ndrangheta boss in Lombardia—said to other men of the 'ndrangheta during an interception on 31 October 2009[25]: *"Calabria, Lombardia, and every other part have agreed pacts and prescriptions, there for everyone [...] if we want things to work out, even when there is some turmoil... we need to think of assembling and not dividing!"*

CONCLUSION

This chapter had three main objectives. First, it has sought to establish the links between certain events in Calabrian history and the evolution of Calabrian mafia clans, the *'ndrine*, indicated with the collective term 'ndrangheta. Second, it has discussed how the clans have evolved on a continuum between tradition and modernity. Tradition is to be found in the maintenance of rituals for affiliation and in the religious attachment to the Madonna di Polsi, the sanctuary where rankings and alliances are approved. Modernity is in the fluidity, the *liquidity* (Forgione 2008) of the clans in exploiting criminal opportunities on the territory. Between modernity and tradition, the clans today exhibit differences across the region but still have similar behaviours in the criminal markets (*'ndranghetism*), as we will see in Part II, and similar structures as the following chapters in this part will show as well.

Third, this chapter has provided an outlook of the contemporary settings of the clans across the region, differentiating them by location and typology and describing what exactly can be grouped under the single name 'ndrangheta and what instead is absorbed within it through an *'ndranghetisation* process. This first chapter has laid out the various elements of the remaining chapters of this book, by focusing on the relationship of the *'ndrine* with their territories, and their control of these territories from politics to economics, from exploitation of social values to exhibition of military power.

NOTES

1. Operation Porto, No. 35/96 + 84/97 R.G.N.R. DDA.
2. Operation Arca, No. 1348/01 R.G.N.R. DDA.
3. Operation Arca, No. 1348/01 R.G.N.R. DDA, p. 14–15.
4. Operation Porto, No. 290/98 + 239/99 R.G.Trib, sentence No.436/2000, p. 124.
5. Operation Porto, No. 290/98 + 239/99 R.G.Trib, sentence No.436/2000, p. 501.
6. Operation Olimpia, No. 104/95 R.G.N.R. DDA + No. 85/96 R.G. GIP DDA + No.15/98 R.G. Court of Assizes sentence No.3/2001 R.G.
7. Operation Olimpia, No. 85/96 R.G. GIP DDA, p. 33.
8. Interview in Reggio Calabria, DDA Procura della Repubblica, 18 April 2013, translated from Italian.
9. Operation Olimpia, sentence No.3/2001 R.G., p. 149.
10. Operation All Inside, No. 9762/11 R.G.N.R. DDA.

11. Operation Crimine, No. 1389/08 R.G.R.N DDA, No. 3655/11 R.G. GIP/GUP, sentence No. 106/12.
12. Operation All Inside II, No. 9762/11 R.G.N.R. DDA, p. 117.
13. Operation Bellu Lavuru, No. 1130/06 R.G.R.N. DDA.
14. Operation Crimine, No. 1389/08 R.G.R.N DDA, No. 3655/11 R.G. GIP/GUP, sentence No. 106/12.
15. Operation Reale, No. 1095/10 R.G.N.R. DDA.
16. A town/city council can be dissolved because of mafia infiltration or collusion under article 143 of law 267/2000. The procedure was firstly introduced in 1991 through law decree 164/1991. It essentially aims at restoring impartiality and good functioning of the town/city administrations through an administrative procedure.
17. Interview in Reggio Calabria, DDA Procura della Repubblica, 16 December 2015, translated from Italian.
18. Operation Crimine, No. 1389/08 R.G.R.N DDA, No. 3655/11 R.G. GIP/GUP, sentence No. 106/12.
19. Operation Armonia, No. 14/1998 R.G.R.N DDA.
20. Operation Cento Anni di Storia, No. 6268/06 R.G.N.R. DDA, p. 20.
21. Interview in Reggio Calabria, DDA Procura della Repubblica, 16 December 2015, translated from Italian.
22. Operation Minotauro, in Piemonte, no. 6161/2007 R.G.N.R. DDA.
23. Operation Crimine, Final Sentence Court No. 106/12 Court of Assizes, Reggio Calabria.
24. Interview in Catanzaro, DDA Procura della Repubblica, 15 December 2015, translated from Italian.
25. Operation Crimine, Final Sentence Court No. 106/12 Court of Assizes, Reggio Calabria, p. 60.

REFERENCES

Arlacchi, P. (1986). *Mafia Business: Mafia ethic and the spirit of capitalism*. London: Verso.

Casaburi, M. (2010). *Borghesia mafiosa. La 'ndrangheta dalle origini ai giorni nostri*. Bari: Dedalo.

Catanzaro, R. (1992). *Men of respect: A social history of the Sicilian Mafia*. New York, Oxford: Maxwell Macmillan International.

Cavaliere, C. (2004). *Un vaso di coccio: dai governi locali ai governi privati : comuni sciolti per mafia e sistema politico istituzionale in Calabria*. Soveria Mannelli: Rubbettino.

Çayli, B. (2010). Social networks of the Italian mafia; the strong and weak parts. *CEU Political Science Journal*, 03, 382–412.

Ciconte, E. (1992). *'Ndrangheta: dall unità a oggi*. Roma: Laterza.

Ciconte, E. (2011). 'Ndrangheta. Soveria Mannelli: Rubbettino.

Ciconte, E. (2013). Politici (e) malandrini. Soveria Mannelli: Rubbettino.

Ciconte, E. (2015). Riti criminali. I codici di affiliazione alla 'ndrangheta. Soveria Mannelli: Rubbettino.

Cingari, G. (1982). Storia della Calabria dall'Unità a Oggi. Bari: Editori Laterza.

Commissione di Accesso. (2012). Relazione, Comune di Reggio Calabria. Rome: Commissione di Accesso al Comune di Reggio Calabria ex art. 143 d.lgs 267/2000.

Cordova, F. (2014). Massoneria in Calabria. Cosenza: Pellegrini Editore.

Coscarelli, A. (1992). Calabria tra sottosviluppo e criminalità mafiosa: analisi del fenomeno criminale con particolare riguardo alle tendenze in atto, alla legislazione antimafia, al ruolo delle istituzioni dello stato e della chiesa in una regione di frontiera. Cosenza: Brenner.

D'Agostini, F. (1972). Reggio Calabria. I moti del luglio 1970—febbraio 1971. Milan: Feltrinelli.

Dalla Chiesa, N. (2010). La convergenza. Mafia e politica nella Seconda Repubblica. Melampo: Milano.

Di Forti, F. (1982). Per una psicoanalisi della mafia: radici, fantasmi, territorio e politica. Verona: G. Bertani.

Dino, A. (2008). La mafia devota: Chiesa, religione. Bari: Editori Laterza.

DNA. (2011). Relazione annuale sulle attività svolte dal Procuratore Nazionale Antimafia e dalla Direzione Nazionale Antimafia nonché sulle dinamiche e strategie della criminalità organizzata di tipo mafioso. Rome: Direzione Nazionale Antimafia.

DNA. (2015). Relazione annuale sulle attività svolte dal Procuratore Nazionale Antimafia e dalla Direzione Nazionale Antimafia nonché sulle dinamiche e strategie della criminalità organizzata di tipo mafioso. Rome: Direzione Nazionale Antimafia.

DNA. (2016). Relazione annuale sulle attività svolte dal Procuratore nazionale e dalla Direzione nazionale antimafia e antiterrorismo nonché sulle dinamiche e strategie della criminalità organizzata di tipo mafioso. Roma: Direzione Nazionale Antimafia e Antiterrorismo.

Fontana, B., & Serarcangeli, P. (1991). L'Italia dei sequestri: dal banditismo sardo alla mafia, dalla 'ndrangheta alla Brigate Rosse, venti anni di storia italiana attraverso i fatti, i nomi, i retroscena della più vergognosa "industria" del nostro paese. Roma: Newton Compton.

Forgione, F. (2008). Relazione Annuale sulla 'Ndrangheta. Roma: Commissione Parlamentare d'inchiesta sul fenomeno della mafi a e sulle altre associazioni criminali.

Gambetta, D. (1993). The Sicilian Mafia: the business of private protection. Cambridge and London: Harvard University Press.

Granovetter, M. S. (1973). The strength of weak ties. American Journal of Sociology, 78(7), 1360–1380.

Guarino, M. (2004). *Poteri segreti e criminalità: l'intreccio inconfessabile tra 'ndrangheta, massoneria e apparati dello Stato.* Bari: Edizioni Dedalo.

Macrì, V., & Ciconte, E. (2009). *Australian 'Ndrangheta.* Soveria Mannelli: Rubbetino.

Malafarina, L. (1981a). *Il Canto della Lupara.* Reggio Calabria: Edizioni Parallelo.

Malafarina, L. (1981b). *L'Operazione Marzano.* Reggio Calabria: Edizioni Parallelo.

Meligrana, M. (1983). Sull'origine e sulla funzione sociale della mafia. In: F. Faeta, LM Lombardi Satriani, P. Martino, et al. (eds.), *Le Ragioni della Mafia. Studi e ricerche di "Quaderni Calabresi".* Milano: Jaca Book.

Mete, V. (2011a). I lavori di ammodernamento dell'autostrada Salerno-Reggio Calabria. Il ruolo delle grandi imprese nazionali. In: R. Sciarrone (ed.), *Alleanze nell'Ombra: Mafie ed economie locali in Sicilia e nel Mezzogiorno.* Roma: Donzelli.

Mete, V. (2011b). Lo Spergiuro di Ippocrate. Mafia, politica e carriere nel campo della sanita' in provincia di Reggio Calabria. In: R. Sciarrone (ed.), *Alleanze nell'Ombra: Mafie ed economie locali in Sicilia e nel Mezzogiorno.* Roma: Donzelli.

Mete, V. (2013). Reggio Calabria tra mafia e dissesto. *Il Mulino, 2,* 201–209.

Nicaso, A., & Gratteri, N. (2012). *Dire e non dire: i dieci comandamenti della 'ndrangheta nelle parole degli affiliati.* Milano: Mondadori.

Paoli, L. (2003). *Mafia brotherhoods: Organized crime, Italian style.* New York and Oxford: Oxford University Press.

Pignatone G., and Prestipino M. (2013). Cosa Nostra e 'ndrangheta: due modelli criminali. In: E. Ciconte, F. Forgione, and I. Sales (eds.), *Atlante delle Mafie. Storia, economia, società, cultura. Volume Secondo.* Soveria Mannelli: Rubbetiino.

Pitaro, V. (1996). *Interviste sulla 'ndrangheta.* Cosenza: Editrice L'Altra Calabria.

Prestifilippo, A. (1998). *A Sud. La Mafia, la 'Ndrangheta, la Massoneria, i Servizi deviati.* Cosenza: Edizioni Memoria.

Sales, I. (2010). *I Preti e i Mafiosi: Storia dei rapporti tra mafie e Chiesa cattolica.* Milano: Dalai Editore.

Sciarrone, R. (2009). *Mafie vecchie, mafie nuove: radicamento ed espansione.* Roma: Donzelli.

Senato della Repubblica. (2015). Relazione sull'Attività svolta e sui Risultati conseguiti dalla Direzione Investigativa Antimafia (Primo Semestre 2014) *Presentatata dal Ministro dell'Interno* 13 January 2015.

Sergi, A. (2015). Mafia and politics as concurrent governance actors. Revisiting political power and crime in Southern Italy. In P. C. Van Duyne, A. Maljević, G. A. Antonopoulos, et al. (Eds.), *The relativity of wrongdoing: Corruption, organised crime, fraud and money laundering in perspective.* Oisterwijk: Wolf Legal Publishers.

Sergi, A., and South, N. (2016). "Earth, Water, Air, and Fire". Environmental Crimes, Mafia Power and Political Negligence in Calabria. In: G. Antonopoulos (ed.), *Illegal Entrepreneurship, 'Organised Crime and Social Control: Essays in Honour of Prof. Dick Hobbs*. New York: Springer.

Sergi, P. (1991). *La 'Santa' Violenta*. Cosenza: Periferia.

Sergi, P. (1993). *Le Mie Calabrie*. Soveria Mannelli: Rubbettino.

Sergi, P. (2013). Il Capoluogo Conteso. Lotte Municipaliste in Calabria all'annuncio del Regionalismo. *Archivio Storico per la Calabria e la Lucania*, *LXXIX*, 135–196.

Teti, V. (2015). *Terra Inquieta*. Soveria Mannelli: Rubbettino.

Trumper, J. B., Maddalon, M., Nicaso, A., et al. (2014). *Male Lingue. Vecchi e Nuovi Codici delle Mafie*. Pellegrini: Cosenza.

Violante, L. (1994). *Non è la Piovra. Dodici tesi sulle mafie italiane*. Torino: Einaudi.

CHAPTER 3

'Ndrangheta Movements in the Centre and North of Italy

Abstract This second chapter of Part I investigates how the criminal model of the 'ndrangheta has moved over the years to a number of regions, replicating peripheral structures but maintaining the direction in Calabria. We will look at Lombardia, Liguria, Piemonte, Emilia Romagna, Lazio, and Veneto as case studies to distinguish between colonisation and delocalisation processes in order to explain the settlement of the clans outside Calabria. Through the analysis of recent investigations, the chapter will focus particularly on transplantation tactics and clans' structures and activities outside their territory of origin.

Keywords Migration • Mafia Colonisation • Mafia Delocalisation • Northern Italy • Central Italy

INTRODUCTION

Throughout its recent history, 'ndrangheta clans have constantly demonstrated an extraordinary capacity to take advantage of the traditional migratory flows, as well as to adapt their economic interests to new emerging opportunities, acting as poly-crime organisations, with an impressive ability of maintaining the difficult equilibrium between localism and globalisation, tradition and innovation. As we will see in this chapter, the criminal behaviour of the 'ndrangheta—the *'ndranghetism*—has been reproduced over the years in a number of regions. Overall, these periph-

© The Editor(s) (if applicable) and The Author(s) 2016
A. Sergi, A. Lavorgna, *'Ndrangheta,*
DOI 10.1007/978-3-319-32585-9_3

eral structures enjoyed a certain degree of autonomy but directives are generally given from Calabria.

Moved by the appetite for the money that was circulating after the economic boom of mid last century, 'ndrangheta clans are deemed to be active in the industrial North since the 1950s, when they slowly started to replace Sicilian groups in their criminal leadership (even if collaborations with the Sicilian mafia and even with Camorra clans continued in later years[1]) up to the point to become the predominant mafia power in the area (Ciconte 2010; Annibaldi and Tocco 2010). The drug market (particularly heroin and cocaine) has been controlled by the Calabrian clans in the northern regions since the 1970s, with the number of mafia-related judicial inquiries into drug crime increased since the 1990s (Ciconte 2010). Already in 1972, sociologists highlighted how drug dealers in the city of Milan were mostly from Calabria and the south of Italy, justifying this with the deprived life conditions of immigrants in the region (Baglivo and Papa 1972). Also kidnappings—more than 150 in Lombardia only— put the 'ndrangheta and especially certain clans from the Reggio Calabria hinterland under the spotlight in the 1970s (Chiavari 2011). While the presence of the 'ndrangheta in the North has been recognised especially in Lombardia and Piemonte because of drug-related crimes, only in more recent years its existence has been acknowledged as a major issue also in other parts of Central and Northern Italy, such as Liguria, Emilia Romagna, Lazio, and Veneto.

After a brief theoretical digression on the two main types of mafia movements—colonisation and delocalisation—as described in criminological literature and by the Italian Antimafia, this chapter will consider the above-mentioned regions as case studies to show the organisational structure and the modus operandi of 'ndranghetisti that moved in other parts of Italy, and the peculiar relationships they maintain with their homeland Calabria.

THEORISING 'NDRANGHETA MOVEMENTS

Outside Calabria, the 'ndrangheta has been at the centre of media and political attention only in the past few years. For a long time, there has been a different political and social perception as well as a different media representation of the phenomenon, with many policy makers who minimised any suggestion of links between politics, economics, and 'ndrangheta clans in the North (Di Ronco and Lavorgna 2016).

Especially over the last decade, however, there has been increasing attention to the presence of the 'ndrangheta in non-traditional mafia territories due to the capacity of different clans to penetrate local socio-economic fabrics (Varese 2006; Lavorgna 2015; Sciarrone 2014). A number of investigations and trials over the last decade have allowed a better understanding of the behaviour and expansion of the clans outside Calabria in their process of *'ndranghetisation*. Specifically, the focus has been on their ability to infiltrate profitable businesses—such as the real estate and the construction sectors—and to create a privileged dialogue with local entrepreneurial class and political elites (Annibaldi and Tocco 2010; Varese 2011; 2006). Operations Crimine-Infinito, Decollo, Minotauro, Alba chiara, La Svolta, Maglio, and Aemilia, among others, as we will see later more in detail, shed light on the presence of the 'ndrangheta in the north of the country (DIA 2014). New methods of investigation and especially the use of electronic surveillance and wiretaps made it possible to gain a better understanding of the 'ndrangheta presence in other parts of Italy.[2] However, as explained by Ilda Boccassini, the public prosecutor of Milan, investigations are sometimes hindered by a problem of *omertà*: despite the worrying number of intimidating incidents, such as arson, complaints are still rare (Lavorgna 2015; Lavorgna 2012a, b).

The organisational structure of this mafia has certainly facilitated the successful *'ndranghetisation* outside Calabria, even when it comes from specific strategic choices (Forgione 2008). Resilient family-based structures and territorial influence allow the clans to have a high degree of organisational freedom and flexibility. The familiar bonds and the kinship ties allow maintaining a strong cultural identity and the reformulation of the *'ndranghetist* behaviour outside the regional boundaries (Paoli 1994; Lavorgna 2015).

The settlement of the clans outside Calabria can be examined through two main prodromic principles: the unintentional resettlement and the voluntary movement of Calabrian communities towards richer regions in search of better working opportunities.

It is estimated that, especially in the 1950s and 1960s, during the period of post-war growth, over a million people migrated from Calabria to the centre and north of Italy (ISTAT 2010). With these migrants, came a number of mafia members (Paoli 1994). Apart from the unintentional resettlement that occurred as part of broader migration movements, *soggiorno obbligato* (forced relocation) was used since the mid-1950s as part of a national criminal policy. As an ancillary form of punishment, *mafiosi* were sent to Central and Northern regions to serve their convictions in the (unsuccessful) attempt to break their links with the criminal associations of their homeland, and to reform their old criminal *mores* by resettling them among law-abiding people. This was an anachronistic choice, which did not properly consider the new possibilities for communication offered in an era of profound technological and social transformation. In fact, contrary to the plans of the Italian government, this relocation—generally not welcomed by the resident population—has been held partially responsible for the expansion of mafia activities, and facilitated the possibility for traditional Southern mafias to establish themselves in new territories (Ciconte 2010). Through chain migration, in fact, family members followed those who had resettled via forced relocation. Probably the most notorious example, Rocco Lo Presti, close to the Mazzaferro clan, was sent in Piemonte with the *soggiorno obbligato* policy in the early 1960s, and soon become a reference point for the 'ndrangheta in the North.[3]

Mafias also follow criminal and economic opportunities. As summarised by Varese (2011), the voluntary movement into a new territory might depend: on the desire to get a specific resource at a lower cost ("resource-seeking" opportunities); on tax convenience or other incentives to reinvest the proceeds of criminal activities in "clean" businesses ("investment-seeking" opportunities); or on the decision to carry out a core criminal activity in a new market ("market-seeking" opportunities). In the case of the 'ndrangheta clans, a specific opportunity to infiltrate certain areas came after the economic boom experienced by Northern Italy, which provided a fertile ground for business (Smuraglia 1994). Also, the considerable number of immigrants in certain urban areas caused a swift and substantial increase of the resident population, which led to an increasing need for housing. New building construction projects were developed, with the consequent need of more manpower. This created and perpetuated a vicious circle between illegal labour, monopolisation of subcontracts, and the hybridisation of 'ndrangheta clans and local entrepreneurs (Annibaldi and Tocco 2010).

For a long time, the movements of the clans in Northern Italy were explained in terms of *colonisation* (Smuraglia 1994) or *transplantation*, defined as *"the ability of a mafia group to offer criminal protection over a sustained period of time outside its region of origin and routine operation"* (Varese 2006: 414). In order to have a successful colonisation, the place of resettlement needs to exhibit certain conditions; in particular, there needs to be availability of resources from the entrepreneurial side, and a certain degree of permeability of services and existing criminal contexts (Dalla Chiesa 2010). According to Varese (2011), mafia transplantation could not occur without a demand for criminal protection, which generally can be found in small territories with low levels of trust among citizens, with newly formed, or booming of, large illegal markets, and without the presence of other illegal local protectors. This model was used, for example, to explain why the 'ndrangheta was able to operate successfully in the small town of Bardonecchia (in Piemonte), while it failed to colonise Verona (in Veneto), where clans were not able to permeate the drug market and civil society effectively mobilised against the clans' attempts to infiltrate the legal economy (Varese 2006).

The colonisation model, however, has to be adjusted to explain the judicially ascertained presence of the 'ndrangheta in other parts of the country. The concepts of *hybridisation* (Licciardi 2011) and *delocalisation* (Sciarrone 2014; Lavorgna 2015) have been used to stress the fact that sometimes clans do not attempt to control (portions of) the territory, but rather subtly infiltrate the socio-economic fabric of the territory of arrival to generate profits to be then moved back to their homeland. Also, recent literature strongly emphasises the collusive role of professionals, entrepreneurs, and politicians as social capital utilised by mafias, "grey areas" where pre-existing illegal behaviours in the new territories favour the existence of new sets of relationships with the newly arrived criminal groups (Sciarrone 2014). Very useful is a further differentiation of mafia expansion as imitation, infiltration, settlement, and hybridisation, where imitation and infiltration are less nuanced and fluid while settlement and hybridisation are more accentuated and advanced forms of penetration in new territories (Sciarrone and Storti 2014).

In the rest of this chapter, we will see how the clans infiltrated different regions of Italy to different extents. Before presenting the cases in terms of colonisation/settlement (Lombardia, Liguria, and Piemonte) or delocalisation/hybridisation (Emilia Romagna, Lazio, and Veneto), however, a preliminary clarification is needed: it is always difficult to pigeonhole complex and evolving phenomena into conceptual categories. The different ways in which the 'ndrangheta has so far penetrated other Italian regions—the *'ndranghetisation* process—can be better interpreted as along a continuum between colonisation and delocalisation.

Colonies in the North

The cases of Lombardia, Liguria, and Piemonte are emblematic to understand the presence of the 'ndrangheta in Northern Italy. In these regions, not only have the clans *imitated* the organisational structures existing in Calabria, but also they *resettled* entire family units, facilitating the territorial expansion of their power and wealth in a *'ndranghetisation* process.

Lombardia

Even if the presence of *'ndrine* in Lombardia has been linked to drug crimes and kidnappings since the 1970s, as emerging from Operations Nord-Sud[4] and Isola Felice,[5] it received relatively little public attention until two major law enforcement investigations in 2010: Crimine and Infinito,[6] carried out in parallel by the Antimafia Prosecutors in Reggio Calabria and Milano. These operations demonstrated the degree that mafia penetration had reached in the region. To borrow the words of the National Antimafia Directorate from Calabria (DNA 2011), Lombardia has indeed been "colonised" by the 'ndrangheta, especially by *'ndrine* from both the west and the east side of Calabria, both in the province of Reggio Calabria and in other provinces (Annibaldi and Tocco 2010).

Lombardia, and specifically the city of Milano, has traditionally enjoyed a core position in the drug market, especially heroin in the 1980s and cocaine later (Commissione Parlamentare d'Inchiesta 2012). Operation Decollo, among others, demonstrated the role of the clans based in the hinterland of Milano in the local distribution of cocaine imported from Calabria or even directly from South America.[7] Milano is also strategic for penetrating legitimate businesses, exploiting public funds, and controlling financial flows (Dalla Chiesa 2010). The construction sector and major infrastructure works are particularly risky: some clans remain in the shadow trying to obtain subcontracts of limited value in activities with low technological expertise, such as the earthmover sector or waste disposal.[8] Other clans try to use a different strategy, by using frontmen for business companies able to run for bigger public tender contracts. For instance, because of both the conspicuous public investments and the international profile, the recent 2015 Exposition (EXPO) in Milano was considered a privileged arena for criminal infiltration. It should be remembered that the problem is not only limited to the Milano area, as demonstrated for instance by operations Wall Street[9] on the 'ndrangheta presence near Lecco, and Isola Felice in the Varese area.[10]

In Lombardia, there is also the problem of increasing political infiltration, which is typical in an area of colonisation: 'ndrangheta members developed a political base through the Calabrian immigrant community, which facilitated the infiltration in local governments (Chiavari 2011; Savatteri 2012). This fact was demonstrated, for instance, by the resignation of the town council of Sedriano (near Milano) in 2013 in the aftermath of the operation Grillo Parlante.[11] To many, the extent of the control of some parts of the territory often paired with a "military" presence (via violent acts) might be surprising. While this is common in the South, in the North clans are generally described as economic-driven forces concerned with the identification of favourable opportunities for the maximisation of their profits (Di Ronco and Lavorgna 2016). However, as stressed in the court order for Operation Cerberus:

> What leaps out is how even the 'entrepreneurial' 'ndrangheta [...] does not give up the military option. The availability of such a vast arsenal is a clear sign of [military] strength and it has an essential deterrence scope in the logic of contraposition and confrontation of the 'ndrangheta families.[12]

Little by little, 'ndrangheta clans became so embedded in the region and its economy that a new mid-level structure (a sort of *mandamento*) called "La Lombardia" was created in the Milano hinterland. The relationship with Calabria has not always been easy to interpret and has been changing over time (DNA 2012). The *'ndrine* gained a certain degree of autonomy, even if the dependence from their homeland remained always strong. Some *'ndranghestisti* even tried to gain more independence and increased autonomy: in 2008 the boss Carmelo Novella attempted to separate the Northern clans from Calabria to create a more autonomous group, but ended up murdered (Savatteri 2012; Lavorgna 2015). Hence, also in Lombardia, hegemonic strategic control is maintained by the clans in Calabria to confirm the consistency and strength of the phenomenon notwithstanding the fluidity of the organisational structure and the successful *'ndranghetisation* process elsewhere.

As anticipated above, Operation Infinito focused on proving the existence and the operational structure of the 'ndrangheta in Lombardia (Calderoni 2015). It demonstrated the presence of the 'ndrangheta in the region as an autonomous body articulated in 15 *locali*, and it also showed how the clans rely on the mafia behaviour and method while maintaining a constant exchange with Calabria. A "chamber of control" (*camera di controllo della Lombardia*) exists to manage problems with the *locali* on spot, leaving them some independence in dealing with members' affiliations and promotions. For instance, in October 2009 for the first time an 'ndrangheta meeting near Milano was caught on camera by law enforcement, filming how new *doti* were given in the area (Chiavari 2011). Also, operation Cerberus showed the existence of a territorial division operating as a consortium among clans in controlling the demolition and earthmover sector in the Milano hinterland,[13] very similar to what happens in Calabria for similar projects. The situation was so consolidated and stable that the entrepreneurs of the area were reported to only have the options either to change job (or area), or to be a victim of extortive behaviours, or to side with the clans.[14]

The infiltration in the socio-economic texture occurred not only via subjugation but also via consensus (DNA 2011). As summarised by the old adagio *"pecunia non olet"* (money does not smell) and demonstrated by the operations Infinito and Tenacia,[15] the pervasiveness of the 'ndrangheta presence in Lombardia occurred often through the collusion of persons connected to the business, administrative, and political sectors, facilitators in the grey zone who cannot be fully considered as part of the 'ndrangheta group but whose activities have been crucial in supporting the success of the criminal organisation (DIA 2014; Chiavari 2011; Dalla Chiesa 2010). The line between this type of connivance and support on one side and full-blown *omertà* and subjection on the other is a thin one: for instance, as reported by Chiavari (2011), of the 199 entrepreneurs involved in the trial for Operation Infinito, only one had actually filed a complaint.

Liguria

In Liguria, the presence of the 'ndrangheta has been reported since the 1960s. In the course of the years, strategic relationships with local politicians were developed and strengthened, as demonstrated for instance by operations La Svolta[16] and Maglio III,[17] which clearly showed how clans were involved in trades of arms and explosives, usury, money laundering, and vote trading, this latter being a stronger indicator of colonisation.

The clans prospered in the wealth of this territory, and the closeness to France has been strategic to keep contacts with fugitives and to carry out businesses in the southern coast of France. As the DDA in Genova notices in Operation Roccaforte, for instance, *"the locale in Ventimiglia becomes also a transit point, where cooperation and relationships with the Calabrian clans in Côte Azure can meet".*[18] Here, in a very complex networking scheme, the clans in Calabria operate *"in continuity"* with their partners in France through the Ligurian connection. As it will be shown in Chap. 4, this appears to apply to almost every other European connection. In Liguria, this occurs through a "chamber of control" in a high position of the hierarchical structure, similar to the one observed in Lombardia (DNA 2012; DNA 2015).

Furthermore, Operation Maglio III clarified even more the structure of the 'ndrangheta clans in Liguria, defined as a *"direct emission"* of Calabrian clans, with whom they *"move in harmony".*[19] It identified four *locali* (in the cities of Genova, Ventimiglia, Lavagna, and Sarzana), each of them with a certain degree of autonomy, but still coordinated with the others, and the one of Genova in a slightly superior position. This, once again, confirms conformity of behaviours without the rigidity of a superimposed structure.

Piemonte

The region of Piemonte, one of the most industrialised areas of the country, has often been under the spotlight for the presence of the 'ndrangheta, and several cases of colonisation have been reported. Clans have been particularly active in drug trafficking,[20] but also in the construction sector, in money laundering, and usury (Annibaldi and Tocco 2010). The city council of Bardonecchia, in the Valsusa valley, was the first one in the north of Italy dissolved for mafia infiltration[21] in 1995.

Piemonte has experienced a significant influx of immigrants since the 1950s. 'Ndrangheta presence has been confirmed in the area with the *soggiorno obbligato* of Rocco Lo Presti and Francesco Mazzaferro, from the Mazzaferro clan from Marina di Gioiosa Ionica on the East coast near Reggio Calabria, who dominated the construction sector in the Bardonecchia area (Varese 2011). Regarding specifically the Valsusa valley, a strong demand for housing started in the 1960s as a consequence of the major expansion in tourism and infrastructures in the area. As explained by Varese (2011), this led to the need for poorly qualified workers, found in the pool of the newly arrived immigrants. Being non-unionised, the construction industries and the workers turned to mafia clans to settle disputes. Along the years, the 'ndrangheta clans were able to secure a conspicuous electoral base in the area (Paoli 1994; Savatteri 2012; Chiavari 2011). Particularly the earthmover sector was used as a source of political influence by the 'ndrangheta, which could rely on an "army" of owner drivers (*"padroncini"*) from their homeland as potential voters and therefore as political leverage tool (Commissione Parlamentare d'Inchiesta 2012). A real control of the territory took place, and also mafia murders were used to this scope, for instance, the assassination in 1983 of Bruno Caccia, the former head prosecutor of Turin who at that time was investigating numerous crimes with alleged 'ndrangheta connection. Only in December 2015 a Calabrian men who currently worked as a baker in Piemonte was arrested for the murder (Neirotti 2015).

More importantly, Operation Minotauro[22] has demonstrated the existence in Piemonte of a colony of the 'ndrangheta formed by nine *locali* hierarchically coordinated by one *Crimine*. There is not in Piemonte a chamber of control like those found in Lombardia and Liguria, but there is one additional territorial structure called *bastarda*, offshoot of one *società* of the *locale* of Bagnara Calabra (near Reggio Calabria), unauthorised from the vertices of the 'ndrangheta but by them tolerated. Still,—in line with the findings of Operation Infinito for Lombardia—the 'ndrangheta is confirmed a phenomenon deeply rooted in Calabria where power concentrates (DNA 2014). In a perfect expression of *glocalism*, and in an intermediary position on the continuum that characterises mafia expansion, 'ndrangheta clans in Piemonte operate by following their *behavioural model*, employing their traditions, rituals, and social practices of communication and leadership, but they also rely on a set of capacities acquired in Piemonte to secure control of key economic activities. As written by the prosecutors of the Operation Minotauro, there is:

A significant situation of *omertà* [...], which is the only explanation of the fact that there have been only a few complaints and even spontaneous complaints, not induced by compelling needs and fears for one's life or that of one's family. Hence, these complaints are often selfish; they are not motivated by the will to let facts emerge, but rather by an attempt to escape [from a bad situation]. They are from someone who, up to that moment, was taking advantage from the closeness to the clans, and that found himself unprepared in dealing with a group so dangerous to be impossible to manage without some institutional help.[23]

The Italian Supreme Court in February 2015 had its final say on Operation Minotauro. With the first definitive sentence making use of article 416-*bis* of the Italian Criminal Code (mafia membership offence) in the north-west of Italy, it certified once and for all the existence of the 'ndrangheta in Torino, with more than 50 persons sentenced for their affiliation to the 'ndrangheta in Piemonte.[24] Similarly, The Italian Supreme Court confirmed the conviction for 19 persons indicted in March 2015— Operation Alba Chiara[25]—demonstrating the presence of 'ndrangheta clans also in the area of Novi Ligure, in the Southern part of Piemonte.

OPPORTUNITIES FOR PROFITS AND DELOCALISATION

As anticipated above, in other parts of Italy—and especially in the north-east and the centre of the country—'ndrangheta clans' settlements are best described in terms of delocalisation. The rest of this chapter will present Emilia Romagna, Lazio, and Veneto as case studies to show different patterns of clans' presence and their modus operandi along a continuum. This framework, however, does not deny the fact that some situations are best described in mixed terms (halfway "colonisation" and "delocalisation", through processes of imitation or hybridisation or infiltration), nor implies the fact that the 'ndrangheta is not present in other regions. For instance, in other central regions such as Toscana, Umbria, and Marche, as reported by Ciconte (2009) among others, 'ndrangheta clans have generally been able to infiltrate the economic texture in a silent and discrete way, without creating any moral panic. Clans have mainly dealt with trafficking of cocaine and heroin, investments in the real estate sector, money laundering, and extortions especially targeting Calabrian entrepreneurs operating in the region (DIA 2014).

Emilia Romagna

In Emilia Romagna, the presence of the 'ndrangheta has been reported since the 1980s and it has been generally considered an example of criminal delocalisation (DIA 2014). Once again, the *soggiorno obbligato* of Antonio Dragone, boss of the clan from Cutro near Crotone, has been considered as the starting point of the replication of mafia models in the area (De Miro 2010). As it was stressed already in Operation Edilpiovra, *"[...] it is evident the awareness of operating in order to meet the goals of criminal mafia-types structures"*.[26] Along the years, investigations showed an increasing interest from the clans towards investments in business companies and especially through the acquisition of legal businesses in touristic areas, extortion and usury, drug trafficking, money laundering, and even illegal betting (SOS Impresa 2008; DIA 2014). The recent interest in Emilia Romagna is probably also linked to the earthquake that stroke the region in 2012, which granted new possibilities to enter in the (re)construction business (DIA 2014). Clans from the Crotone area, such as the Vrenna-Bonaventura and Grande Aracri clans, have traditionally been very active especially in the areas around Reggio Emilia, Modena, Parma, and Piacenza (DNA 2012) with the clan Grande Aracri becoming a very interesting case of national and international mafia expansion as we will see also in the next chapter. Overall they tried to operate under the radar, with the exception of a blood feud in Reggio Emilia between different families in the late 1990s (De Miro 2010).

It is interesting to note that also in delocalisation cases infiltration in the socio-economic texture occurred not only via subjugation but also via consensus. As it emerges, for instance, from Operation Pandora,[27] the traditional relationship based on the inferiority and subjection of entrepreneurs towards the criminal actors has evolved in a way that favours the formers. Entrepreneurs are not always merely "victims", but some of them have became collaborators or even associates to the clans; not only do they receive loans, but they also proactively involve the 'ndranghetisti in new and other collaborative entrepreneurial activities for money laundering.

The presence and the modus operandi of the 'ndrangheta in Emilia Romagna have been further clarified in the course of the recent Operation Aemilia,[28] which demonstrated that there is a real settlement—and not only infiltration—of clans in the area. Even though investigations mainly refer to one clan in Calabria (Grande Aracri), the operation led to the arrest of 160 people, among which the alleged boss of the Reggio Emilia clans. Evidence suggests also that around Reggio Emilia a new clan had developed, autonomous from the Grande Aracri one from Cutro (near Crotone) from which it originated, able to develop relationships not only with the entrepreneurial world but also with politics and the media (DNA 2016). As we said before, the continuum from colonisation and delocalisation evolves and constantly swings from one to the other. Initially an example of delocalisation, Emilia Romagna is today closer to the colonisation model.

Lazio

In Lazio the presence of the 'ndrangheta has been recorded since the 1970s, with clans especially from the areas of Reggio Calabria and Vibo

Valentia. In a region where there is the presence of both other mafias and smaller but very violent groups, the clans have demonstrated to be able to cooperate with other criminal networks, being focused more on their financial interests rather than on the control of the territory (Cabras 1994; Lavorgna 2012a, b).

'Ndrangheta clans have been particularly active in taking over commercial businesses in the city centre of Rome for money laundering purposes. In recent years, law enforcement confiscated several commercial businesses because of infiltration of clans linked to the Piromalli, Molè, and Alvaro clans[29] from the area of Gioia Tauro: among others, the Antico Caffè Chigi, often attended by politicians because of its location near the Prime Minister's office, and the Cafè de Paris—immortalised in Fellini's movie *La Dolce Vita*—that was seized together with other real estate assets in July 2009 (and partially released from seizure in 2015). Also, the *'ndrine* in Rome showed a great ability to accumulate and exploit social and institutional capital through active cooperation with individuals in different roles in society. This proved successful as links with Calabrian clans were found in the so-called Operation Mondo di Mezzo,[30] investigating on a system of relationships between an autonomous criminal group—called Mafia Capitale—and politicians, bureaucrats, public officials, and public servants in strategy of the former to penetrate public administration in the capital city (Sergi 2015; Sergi 2016). With Dalla Chiesa (2015) we can agree upon an evolution of mafia settlements in Rome, not linked to the control of territory as a physical entity, but rather intended as penetration in institutions and portions, enclaves, of the city; this seems valid for both the Mafia Capitale group and for 'ndrangheta clans.

In Lazio the penetration of Calabrian clans can be read as a case of *hybridisation* with local criminal groups. Besides Rome, clans settled in the coastal area have been involved, among other things, in drug trafficking. Also, fugitives have been found living in the region (DIA 2014). While so far a *locale* has not been identified—which explains our choice to broadly categorise the presence of *'ndranghetisti* in Lazio as a case of delocalisation—the situation in Lazio has been described as "*critical*" (DNA 2012: 130) especially in the aftermath of Operation Mondo di Mezzo, whose trial in Spring 2016 is ongoing. The hypothesis is that the significant presence of Calabrian immigrants in the area might have disguised the settlement of a more structured presence of the 'ndrangheta in the area, as it has been suggested in recent investigations. For instance, as reported in the latest Antimafia Report (DNA 2015: 43), in 2013 the Velletri Court in the

Rome hinterland for the first time recognised the existence in the coastal area of Lazio of a *'ndrina*—in this case separated from the clan Gallace from Guardavalle (in the Catanzaro hinterland)—that, however, replicates the clan's organisation in Calabria, while maintaining a certain degree of autonomy also in affiliation choices. The investigation was also related to the dissolution for mafia infiltration of the city council of Nettuno, a town on the coastal area near Rome, in 2005, which emphasises the relationships clans have been developing with local administrations.

Veneto

Only in recent years the presence of 'ndrangheta clans has been recognised as a key issue also in the north-east of the country. The region of Veneto provides a good case study. This region has in fact been described at high risk of mafia infiltration, especially by clans from Lamezia Terme and Crotone (Pennisi 2012). After all, the relative wealth of the region and especially of the areas around Padova, Venezia, and Verona already attracted the attention of other local and international criminal groups. However, most people living in the area for a long time did not think of mafia as a significant problem in Veneto (Demos&Pi—Osservatorio sul Nord-Est 2010; Lavorgna 2012a, b). The presence of the 'ndrangheta in the region was reportedly overlooked also because of the presence of Camorra clans from Campania in the area, and the assumption that co-existence would have been difficult (Lavorgna et al. 2013). This interpretation ignored the fact that Veneto is indeed an area of delocalisation for mafias (Pennisi 2012), and therefore groups are not interested in the capillary control of the territory. On the contrary, also in this case 'ndrangheta clans showed to be open to, and able to, cooperate with other criminal organisations (DIA 2014).

Historically, also the Veneto has received mafia members because of the *soggiorno obbligato* policy, especially since the late 1960s and in the 1970s (CROSS 2014). However, differently from Lombardia and Piemonte, Veneto never experienced the massive migration from Southern Italy during the economic boom, as in those years the economy of the region was still developing and struggling to stabilise. In fact, for a long time, Veneto suffered from poverty and emigration because of its poor agricultural economy. Only after the Second World War the region slowly developed a peculiar model of economic growth based on small and medium enterprises, for the most part concentrated in specific parts of the territory and specialised in certain industrial sectors, commerce, and tourism. Some of these economic activities are traditionally an easy target for criminal groups.

However, Veneto had never been considered at major risk from organised crime infiltration until the recession began to affect the region's economy. High levels of unemployment, lack of economic investments, and reduced availability of bank loans made the system permeable to criminal economies especially for money laundering. An increasing number of cases have shown that some 'ndrangheta clans took advantage of this situation: because of the money liquidity enjoyed from drug trafficking, they exploited a fertile ground for usury, for real estate investments during the slowdown in property prices, and for the takeover of vulnerable business activities. Also, in order to maintain their contracts, some companies started working below cost and ended up asking for financial help to criminal organisations. The clans had a certain appeal for local businesses and, in practice, were seen as a valid alternative when legal sources were insufficient or not available (Lavorgna 2015). It is worth noting that, as regards drug trafficking in the area, the clans tend to take care only of the large-scale aspects of the trade, leaving local distribution to local and ethnic groups (Smuraglia 1994), again confirming their ability to successfully co-exist with others.

In Veneto, the 'ndrangheta is confirmed as *poly-crime* group. For instance, in the province of Verona, several investigations—such as operations Panama, Hydra, Dirty Investments, and Porto Franco—led to the arrest of 'ndrangheta members (mostly linked to the Piromalli, Pesce, and Molé clans from Gioia Tauro, and the Vrenna, Ciampà, and Bonaventura clans from Crotone) for trafficking of arms, weapons and explosives, exploitation of public tenders, extortion, money laundering, and real estate investments. Also, other operations—such as Scacco Matto and Libra—affecting the Padova area led to the arrests of *'ndranghetisti* from the Reggio Calabria and Vibo Valentia area (Lavorgna 2015).

The *'ndranghetisation* process in Veneto is indeed made of all different *'ndranghete*. Even if Veneto at the moment is a clear example of delocalisation, according to Osservatorio Ambiente e Legalità Venezia (Legambiente Veneto 2013) in recent years the situation is getting closer to the one experienced in colonisation areas, with a more stable and continuous presence and connivance not only of the entrepreneurial but also of the political world.

CONCLUSION

The cases introduced in this chapter present a complex and evolving scenario as regards the presence and the structures of the 'ndrangheta in Italy. What remains constant in all the cases considered is the interdependence between what happens in the "new" territories and what occurs in Calabria

(Sciarrone 2014). Keeping this in mind, it has to be acknowledged that, outside Calabria, all 'ndrangheta clans have demonstrated an ability to adapt to new territories and better exploit crime opportunities to increase their efficiency. From a prosecution point of view, this ability to adapt has caused severe difficulties: outside Calabria, the big problem for Antimafia prosecutors has often been to establish whether the entrepreneurial approach and the hybrid methods used by the 'ndrangheta clans in other parts of Italy are enough to qualify the criminal actors involved as members of the mafia-type criminal associations according to article 416-*bis* of the Italian Criminal Code. This is true especially when there was not a clear control of the territory and the *mafia behaviour* was not fully reflecting the traditional, even stereotyped, characteristics that we find in mafia homelands (Annibaldi and Tocco 2010; Lavorgna and Sergi 2014). The development of *'ndranghetism* traits and the process of *'ndranghetisation* of the clans in the north and centre of Italy remains however undeniable.

This chapter also demonstrated that, even if it is useful to distinguish between two or more mafia styles of movements (colonisation and delocalisation or settlement and hybridisation), 'ndrangheta clans seem to move across a more fluid continuum, depending on evolving characteristics of the territories of arrival as well as events in Calabria. Probably, this started years ago and has now begun to be recognised by recent law enforcement investigations. It cannot, therefore, be excluded that clans might change strategy and carry out activities with higher social impact outside their homeland (DIA 2014). In any case, the fate of non-traditional areas appear tightly linked to Calabrian evolution. In the traditional areas, in fact, a third generation of *'ndranghetisti* might be able to modify and modernise the modus operandi used so far, up to the point to completely replace the local entrepreneurial class in certain sectors (Dalla Chiesa 2010). In areas of delocalisation or hybridisation, recent investigations show a trend of stabilisation of the clans and of political infiltration that can also suggest a situation getting closer to more pervasive colonisation mechanisms. In both cases, infiltration has been at least partially allowed by the connivance, aware or unaware, of part of the local population.

Notes

1. See, for instance, Operation Decollo, No. 1779-6541/2001-3164/2002-1429/2003 R.G.N.R. DDA + 2523-8748/2001-2085-2086/2003 R.G. G.I.P., p. 26. For Cosa Nostra, Operation Pavone 4, No. 01/2006 + 8042/2007 R.G. GIP.

2. Operation Decollo, No. 1779-6541/2001-3164/2002-1429/2003 R.G.N.R. DDA + 2523-8748/2001 – 2085-2086/2003 R.G. GIP, p. 25.
3. Lo Presti-Arcuri, Supreme Court, Sez. I, sentence No. 3602, 2009.
4. Operation Nord-Sud, No. 443/93 R.G.N.R. DDA.
5. Operation Isola Felice, No. 4480/93 R.G. GIP.
6. Operation Infinito, No. 43733/06 R.G.N.R., No. 8265/06 R.G. GIP + Reggio Calabria Appeal Court sentence, 27.2.2014 + Supreme Courte sentence, Sez IV, 6.6.2014.
7. Operation Decollo, No. 1779-6541/2001 – 3164/2002–1429/2003 R.G.N.R. DDA + 2523-8748/2001 – 2085-2086/2003 R.G. GIP, p. 24.
8. Operation Fly Hole, No. 43733/06 R.G.N.R. and No. 8265/06 R.G. GIP.
9. Operation Wall Street, No. 12602/92.21 R.G.N.R. DDA + No. 23/94 Court of Assizes. + 24/94, + 27/94 + 32/94 + 1/95 + 2/92.
10. Operation Isola Felice, No. 4480/93 R.G. GIP.
11. Operation Grillo Parlante, No. 73990/10 R.G.N.R. + No 14548/10 R.G. GIP.
12. Operation Cerberus, No. 41849/07 R.G.N.R DDA + No. 8183/07 R.G. GIP, p. 2010.
13. Operation Cerberus, No. 41849/07 R.G.N.R DDA + No. 8183/07 R.G. GIP.
14. Operation Cerberus, No. 41849/07 R.G.N.R DDA + No. 8183/07 R.G. GIP, pp. 225–226.
15. Operations Infinito, Court decision No. 5339/14, No. 6152/2013 RGA.
16. Operation La Svolta, No. 9028/10/21 R.G.N.R. DDA.
17. Operation Maglio III, No. 2268/10/21 R.G.N.R. DDA + No. 4644/11 R.G. GIP.
18. Operation Roccaforte, No. 12188/05/21 R.G.N.R. DDA, p. 68.
19. Operation Maglio III, No. 2268/10/21 R.G.N.R DDA + No. 4644/11 R.G.GIP, p. 9.
20. Operation Cartagine, No.533/94 R.G.N.R. DDA.
21. A town/city council can be dissolved because of mafia infiltration or collusion under article 143 of law 267/2000. The procedure was firstly introduced in 1991 through law decree 164/1991.
22. Operation Minotauro, No. 6191/2007 R.G.N.R. DDA.
23. Operation Minotauro, No. 6191/2007 R.G.N.R. DDA + 4775/09 R.G. GIP, p. 1271.
24. Operation Minotauro, Supreme Court, II sez.pen., 23.02.2015.
25. Operation Alba chiara, No. 8928/11 R.G.N.R DDA.
26. Operation Edilpiovra, No. 398/03 R.G. GIP + No. 5754/02 R.G.N.R. DDA p. 46.
27. Operation Pandora, No. 11322/06/21.
28. Operation Aemilia, No. 8846/15 R.G.R.N. DDA + No. 10788/15 R.G.R.N. DDA + 11697/15 R.G.R.N. DDA + 12240/15 R.G.R.N. DDA.

29. Operation Bucefalo, No. 2463/2009 R.G.R.N. DDA + No.1401/2010 R.G.R.N. DDA + No. 8/2015 R.G.R.N. DDA.
30. Operation Mondo di Mezzo, No. 30456/10 R.G.N.R. DDA.

References

Annibaldi, P., & Tocco, M. (2010). *L'infiltrazione della criminalità organizzata nell'economia di alcune regioni del Nord Italia*. Roma: CNEL.

Baglivo, A., & Papa, S. (1972). *Il fenomeno migratorio oggi. Conferme e prospettive*. Milano: C.O.I.

Cabras, P. (1994). *La situazione della criminalità organizzata a Roma e nel Lazio. Commissione parlamentare di inchiesta sul fenomeno della mafia e sulle altre associazioni criminali simili*. Roma: Camera dei Deputati Senato della Repubblica.

Calderoni, F. (2015). Predicting organized crime leaders. In: G. Bichler, and A. E. Malm (eds) *Disrupting criminal networks. Network analysis in crime prevention*. Boulder: Lynne Rienner Publishers.

Chiavari, M. (2011). *La quinta mafia. Come e perché la mafia al Nord oggi è fatta anche da uomini del Nord*. Milano: Salani.

Ciconte, E. (2009). *La criminalità organizzata in Toscana. Storia, caratteristiche ed evoluzione*. Firenze: Regione Toscana.

Ciconte, E. (2010). *'Ndrangheta Padana*. Soveria Mannelli: Rubbettino.

Commissione Parlamentare d'Inchiesta. (2012). *Relazione territoriale sulle attività illecite connesse al ciclo dei rifiuti nella regione Lombardia*. Roma: Camera dei Deputati, Senato della Repubblica, XVI Legislatura.

CROSS. (2014). *Primo rapporto trimestrale sulle aree settentrionali per la Presidenza della Commissione parlamentare di inchiesta sul fenomeno mafioso*. Milano: Università degli Studi di Milano.

Dalla Chiesa, N. (2010). *La convergenza. Mafia e politica nella Seconda repubblica*. Melampo: Milano.

Dalla Chiesa N. (2015). A proposito di Mafia Capitale. Alcuni Problemi Teorici. *CROSS. Rivista di Studi e Ricerche sulla Criminalità Organizzata*. 1(2): DOI: 10.13130/cross-16634.

De Miro, A. (2010). Commissione Parlamentare di inchiesta sul fenomeno della mafia e sulle altre associazioni criminali, anche straniere. Prefettura di Reggio Emilia. *Relazione del Prefetto di Reggio Emilia*. Reggio Emilia: Ufficio Territoriale del Governo.

Demos&Pi—Osservatorio sul Nord-Est. (2010). Criminalità organizzata e criminalità comune: i timori del Nord Est. *Il Gazzettino* 30 November

Di Ronco, A., and Lavorgna, A. (2016). Changing representations of organized crime in the Italian press. *Trends in Organised Crime*. (Online first, DOI 10.1007/s12117-016-9270-7).

DIA. (2014). Attività Svolta e Risultati Conseguiti dalla Direzione Investigativa Antimafia, Luglio-Dicembre 2014. *Relazione del Ministro dell'Interno al Parlamento*. Roma: Direzione Investigativa Antimafia.

DNA. (2011). *Relazione annuale sulle attività svolte dal Procuratore Nazionale Antimafia e dalla Direzione Nazionale Antimafia nonché sulle dinamiche e strategie della criminalità organizzata di tipo mafioso*. Roma: Direzione Nazionale Antimafia.

DNA. (2012). *Relazione annuale sulle attività svolte dal Procuratore Nazionale Antimafia e dalla Direzione Nazionale Antimafia nonché sulle dinamiche e strategie della criminalità organizzata di tipo mafioso*. Roma: Direzione Nazionale Antimafia.

DNA. (2014). *Relazione annuale sulle attività svolte dal Procuratore Nazionale Antimafia e dalla Direzione Nazionale Antimafia nonché sulle dinamiche e strategie della criminalità organizzata di tipo mafioso*. Roma: Direzione Nazionale Antimafia.

DNA. (2015). *Relazione annuale sulle attività svolte dal Procuratore Nazionale Antimafia e dalla Direzione Nazionale Antimafia nonché sulle dinamiche e strategie della criminalità organizzata di tipo mafioso*. Roma: Direzione Nazionale Antimafia.

DNA. (2016). *Relazione annuale sulle attività svolte dal Procuratore nazionale e dalla Direzione nazionale antimafia e antiterrorismo nonché sulle dinamiche e strategie della criminalità organizzata di tipo mafioso*. Roma: Direzione Nazionale Antimafia e Antiterrorismo.

Forgione, F. (2008). *Relazione Annuale sulla 'Ndrangheta*. Roma: Commissione Parlamentare d'inchiesta sul fenomeno della mafia e sulle altre associazioni criminali.

ISTAT. (2010). Immigration and emigration from/to other Italian Municipalities and internal migration balance (a) by region and geographical area -Years 1902–2009. *Times Series*. Roma: Istituto Nazionale di Statistica.

Lavorgna A. (2012, January). Family Planning: the Calabrian mafia spreads northwards in Italy. *Jane's Intelligence Review*, 42–47.

Lavorgna A. (2012, April). Capital Crime: Gang violence returns to Rome. *Jane's Intelligence Review*. 2–5.

Lavorgna, A. (2015). La 'ndrangheta migrante si espande a Nord Est. *Giornale di Storia Contemporanea, XVIII*(1): 45–63.

Lavorgna, A., Lombardo, R., & Sergi, A. (2013). Organised Crime in Three Regions: Comparing the Veneto, Liverpool and Chicago. *Trends in Organized Crime, 16*(3), 265–285.

Lavorgna, A., & Sergi, A. (2014). Types of organised crime in Italy. The multifaceted spectrum of Italian criminal associations and their different attitudes in the financial crisis and in the use of Internet technologies. *International Journal of Law, Crime and Justice, 42*(1), 16–32.

Legambiente Veneto. (2013) 'Ndrangheta, corruzione e cemento. Il Veneto che deve cambiare. *Osservatorio Ambiente e Legalità Venezia* Venezia: Legambiente Veneto.

Licciardi, G. (2011). La Mafia in Veneto. Un'ibridazione criminale lunga trent'anni. In S. Palidda & M. Sanfilippo (Eds.), *Emigrazione e organizzazioni criminali.* Edizioni Sette Città: Viterbo.

Neirotti, M. (2015). Bruno Caccia, il giudice che aveva capito tutto. *La Stampa* 23 December (http://www.lastampa.it/2015/12/23/italia/cronache/quel-giudice-che-aveva-capito-tutto-eRGPDHItp5eZ1d5wU1nRjK/pagina.html).

Paoli, L. (1994). An underestimated criminal phenomenon: The Calabrian 'Ndrangheta. *European Journal of Crime, Criminal Law and Criminal Justice, 3*, 212–238.

Pennisi, R. (2012). Audizione del Sostituto Procuratore Nazionale Antimafia, Dottor Roberto Pennisi. Roma: 104a seduta Senato della Repubblica—Camera dei Deputati XL.

Savatteri G. (2012) *Il Contagio. Come la 'Ndrangheta ha infettato l'Italia.* Bari: Laterza.

Sciarrone, R. (2014). Tra sud e nord. Le mafie nelle aree non tradizionali. In: R. Sciarrone (ed) *Mafie al Nord. Strategie criminali e contesti locali.* Roma: Donzelli Editore.

Sciarrone, R., & Storti, L. (2014). The territorial expansion of mafia-type organized crime. The case of the Italian mafia in Germany. *Crime, Law and Social Change, 61*(1), 37–60.

Sergi, A. (2015, 11 November). The Mafia Mega Trial that has Italy on Tenterhooks. *Newsweek Europe.* (http://europe.newsweek.com/mafia-mega-trial-that-has-italy-tenterhooks-336366?rx=eu).

Sergi, A. (2016a). A proposito di Mafia Capitale. Spunti per tipizzare il fenomeno mafioso nei sistemi di common law". *Rivista di Studi e Ricerche sulla criminalità organizzata, 2*(1), 96–116. Open Access http://riviste.unimi.it/index.php/cross/article/view/6974.

Smuraglia, C. (1994). *Relazione sulle risultanze dell'attività del gruppo di lavoro incaricato di svolgere accertamenti su insediamenti e infiltrazioni di soggetti e organizzazioni mafiose in aree non tradizionali.* Roma: Camera dei Deputati Senato della Repubblica.

SOS Impresa. (2008). *Le mani della criminalità sulle imprese. XI rapporto,* Roma: Confesercenti SOS Impresa.

Varese, F. (2006). How Mafias migrate: the case of the 'Ndrangheta in Northern Italy. *Law & Society Review, 40*(2), 411–444.

Varese, F. (2011). *Mafias on the move: how organized crime conquers new territories.* Princeton, NJ, Oxford: Princeton University Press.

CHAPTER 4

'Ndrangheta Movements Around the World

Abstract Following from the previous chapter, this fourth and conclusive chapter of Part I shall look at the presence of 'ndrangheta clans outside of Italy. It will present and describe the importance of family ties and migration routes for 'ndrangheta settlements, with the specific cases of Germany and Switzerland in Europe and, outside of Europe, with reference to the cases of Canada and Australia. In particular, this chapter shall look at different movements of 'ndrangheta clans, their structures and their relationships with Calabrian clans, and their activities and their reputation abroad.

Keywords European Organised Crime • Germany • Australia • Canada • Switzerland

Introduction

This chapter will address the link between migration and mafia movements outside of Italy. Movements abroad are made more problematic not only because of the geographical distances but also because the presence of 'ndrangheta clans can lead to an improper and unjust labelling of migrants from Calabria, even more than in the rest of Italy.

First, this chapter will look at Calabrian migration outside of Italy, mostly focusing on historical migration. This is a necessary exercise to specify that the link between 'ndrangheta and Calabrian migration is *not* automatic: colonisation has *not* occurred in every territory with a significant

© The Editor(s) (if applicable) and The Author(s) 2016
A. Sergi, A. Lavorgna, *'Ndrangheta,*
DOI 10.1007/978-3-319-32585-9_4

presence of Calabrian migrants. However, the opposite is not true: when-ever we find a substantial settlement of the 'ndrangheta there is a connec-tion with migrant communities from Calabria, as it is the case for Canada and Australia. Second, this chapter will look at the confused—because too contemporary—situation in Europe, and will focus on Germany and Switzerland as case studies in the continent.

CALABRIAN MIGRATION AND MAFIA MIGRATION OUTSIDE OF ITALY

As seen in the previous chapter, criminological studies of migration have already demonstrated the nexus between migration and organised crime, either in terms of criminal activities committed against migrants or of migrant criminals (Arsovska 2015). When it comes to the 'ndrangheta clans, as seen in the previous chapter, the situation is complicated by the high numbers of migrants from Calabria, which has been a constituent and constant factor in the evolution of the region especially in between the World Wars (Cingari 1982). However, Calabrians have moved also in the first decades of the last century. Following their movements across the globe is not an easy task, due to the lack of reliable and comprehen-sive sources and the different methods of collection of data at national levels (Ministero degli Affari Esteri 2005). There is a tendency, especially abroad, to assume the preservation of culture, values, and identities of Calabrian origin, without measuring the effect of the conditions of arrival and after the arrival of migrants (Franzina 1998).

According to Europol, 'ndrangheta clans are today present in Spain, France, Belgium, the Netherlands, Germany, Switzerland, Canada, the USA, Colombia, and Australia (Europol 2013: 3). Europol (2013: 11) notices how *"consolidated and better integrated immigrant communi-ties of Calabrians all over the world provided fertile ground for external offshoots of the criminal organisation"*. We cannot, however, overlap the geography of *'ndrine* or *locali* of the 'ndrangheta with the destinations of Calabrian migrants abroad. There is *"no automatic link"* between the presence of *"migrants arriving from areas with a strong mafia presence and criminal settlements"* (DNA 2012: 109). For example, we do not find, in Antimafia investigations, enduring links between 'ndrangheta clans in Calabria and clans settled in Argentina, even though the migration of Calabrians to Argentina has been notoriously massive, with Argentina having the largest Italian (and Calabrian) community of migrants even today (Fondazione Migrantes 2014). Similarly in Europe, notwithstanding considerable migration to the UK, we do have only sporadic events linked to mafia groups (Allum 2013; Campana 2013). However, we cannot deny that among Calabrian migrants some were and are honest citizens while others have or had mafia skills (Varese 2011).

The Italian National Institute of Statistics has tracked the migration from every Italian region towards different countries of destinations—France, Germany, Switzerland, Canada, the USA, Argentina, Brazil, and Australia—since the unification of Italy (ISTAT 2007a, b). Even though it is quite difficult to isolate exact figures—especially considering the numbers of returns to Italy each year—it is very visible from these statistics how migration from Calabria has been steady and consistent towards these countries, with higher numbers at the beginning of the century (1901–1914, with a peak of 62,290 people migrated in 1905) and after the Second World War (1949–1966, with a peak of 38,080 in 1957).

When following Calabrian migrants outside of Italy, also today's numbers are indicative. In 2014, there are 375,805 Calabrians abroad recorded by the AIRE (Association of Italian Residents Abroad) (Fondazione Migrantes 2014: 5). Calabria is the fourth region of migrants from Italy after Sicily, Campania, and Lazio, which is relevant in proportion to the overall dimension of the region, which only counts around two million people. About 18 % of Calabrians live abroad (Fondazione Migrantes 2014). Migrants of today from Calabria to Europe choose primarily the UK, Germany, Switzerland, and France (ISTAT 2014). Outside of Europe, countries of choice are Argentina, Canada, the USA, and Australia (Fondazione Migrantes 2014). This seems to be partially in line with historical routes of migration (Sergi 2013).

It needs to be always kept in mind that, differently from migration towards Central and Northern Italy, migration abroad also means calculations of convenience based not only on job opportunities but also on the possibility to obtain a visa to stay. This is certainly valid today (Bernardotti 2015), but, *mutatis mutandis*, it was valid decades ago too and it still marks the difference between migration to European countries and migration outside of Europe. Geography and costs of transportation historically played a role in the choice of the initial destination for migrants especially from the south of Italy, where poverty levels were higher (Del Boca and Venturini 2003). Similarly, in *"non-contiguous territories"*, as specified by Varese (2011: 6), the ability of a mafia group to operate over a significant period of time and in one or more illegal trades depends, and depended upon different factors. Migration is one of these factors, but not the only one; others could be strategic movements to escape prosecution or mafia wars, and more lenient repression policies of the country of arrival. Furthermore, the social, structural, and technological changes occurred in the past decades have obviously affected the way Calabrian clans have kept contacts, or resumed contacts, with their representatives or their families abroad. Logically, especially abroad, generational changes and specific country's conditions affect the way mafia families of today can exploit the links with migrants (even when related by blood or mafia affiliation) of yesterday.

When differentiating between phenomena of delocalisation and colonisation abroad, we need to clarify a preliminary point. Europe, apart from certain specific areas, such as Germany—as we will see later on in this chapter—is primarily placed on the delocalisation side of our mafia movement continuum. Other countries outside Europe that experienced '*ndranghetisation* processes (especially linked to drugs trafficking, as we will see in Chap. 5 of this book) have been stage for colonisation in at least two known cases (Australia and Canada). Indeed, migration outside of Europe is relevant for mafia settlements especially when looking at pre-War and post-War periods: the time and difficulty to travel back to the motherland made migrant communities more *static* and cultural identities of origin more crystallised in the places of arrival, with different levels and timings of assimilation and integration (Del Boca and Venturini 2003). Conversely, migration within Europe is certainly more *mobile*, especially today, and this is also true for mafia movements, with a constant exchange, dynamism of cultures, and shifting of national and regional identities often more towards integration and multiculturalism than assimilation (O'Reilly 2007).

THE EUROPEAN REACH

In 2012 the National Antimafia Directorate, for the first time after Operation Crimine,[1] has presented in a comprehensive manner the articulations of 'ndrangheta clans internationally. The DNA has identified the unique ability of the Calabrian clans to move around the globe and to create different types of bonds with Calabrian migrants as well as with other local organised crime groups (DNA 2012). In 2012, the DNA (2012: 109) also noticed that of the overall presence of Calabrian migrants abroad, around 50 % are in Europe and the other 50 % outside of Europe. The countries of destination and residency in Europe are (in order) Germany,

Switzerland, France, and Belgium. When it comes to the main countries where the 'ndrangheta operates in Europe, we find Germany, Switzerland, Spain, the Netherlands, Belgium, France, and also some areas in Eastern Europe in line with the study by Europol (DNA 2014; Europol 2013). The overlapping between migration routes and mafia migration in Europe seems, therefore, only partial. While for Germany, and Switzerland to a lesser extent, we might see a more stable and incisive proliferation of the clans—in forms closer to the colonisation model—in Spain, France, the Netherlands, Belgium, and Eastern Europe the pattern seems to be mostly one of delocalisation, where the clans outsource some activities to local groups and interact with them for activities linked to other illicit trafficking, especially, but not only, drugs.

In terms of activities, next to illegal "classics" (drugs and money laundering) researchers and investigations have found legal investments as well, such as restaurants, food supply stores, real estate, and hotels (Caneppele and Sarno 2013). Recent research has also found that money laundering activities abroad are not as common and widespread as intuitively thought (Calderoni et al. 2015), which could be a sign that investments are still mainly kept in Calabria and Italy. The type of activity the clans engage in can also give some very preliminary indication on the type of their settlement abroad. In fact, as we will see later in more details, in Germany the clans are more strategically submerged into the legal economy, as their settlement is more stable and long lasting. In countries like Spain, Belgium, or France, the clans appear predominantly involved in illegal activities together with local groups, as also indicated by the number of arrests of fugitives from Calabria in those countries (Caneppele and Sarno 2013): delocalisation seems more common and convenient than colonisation. This is not a clear-cut indication, quite the opposite. As often is the case with the 'ndrangheta clans, structures and networks are much more fluid and based on different factors, including both strategic calculations and transient opportunities for the clans.

A number of Antimafia operations have confirmed the existence of various forms of 'ndrangheta presence across Europe. A request of the DIA in Imperia (Liguria) dated May 2011[2] explains how 'ndrangheta members had opened a number of channels among Spain, France, Milano in Lombardia, Torino in Piemonte, and Calabria, through Liguria, to make sure they had access to the best and the cheapest cocaine on the market. Operation Mauser[3] proved the existence of a trafficking ring in Rosarno (in the West coast of Reggio Calabria, near Vibo Valentia), and individuals in the Netherlands and Germany. In the course of this operation, the authorities of the three countries arrested 16 people while at the same time observing some internal dynamics of the Calabrian clan involved whose members were indicted also for kidnapping, slavery, and murder. Among others, Operations Acero[4] in Reggio Calabria and Krupy[5] in Rome, have demonstrated the ability of clans from Siderno, in the East coast of Reggio Calabria (known for their Canada–Australia connection, as we will see later on in this chapter), to diversify their activities (drugs and money laundering) in the Netherlands (through the flower and stolen chocolate industries, see Chap. 6) and in Canada.

Aside from illegal activities, which will be the object of a more detailed analysis in Chap. 6, the expansion of the '*ndrine* in Europe poses questions on their structure and their organisational arrangements. How much do the clans adapt to the country of destination? How much the contact with other local criminal realities affects their structure? All the latest operations in Europe have indicated a fast evolution in the organisational structure of 'ndrangheta clans, but at the same time have confirmed that the core remains the behavioural model—which we called '*ndranghetism* in the Introduction to this book—made of intimidation, reputation, violence, and exploitation of social and cultural Calabrian values and ties. Notwithstanding successful '*ndranghetisation* processes, the core of mafia behaviour also in Europe remains the "traditional" 'ndrangheta even when investigators abroad deny or misunderstand the involvement of the Calabrian clans. For example, this is confirmed in Operation Krupy. In this operation—which follows trafficking of drugs and chocolate back and forth from Lazio, Calabria, and the Netherlands in a very functional network involving Calabrian, Neapolitan, and Albanian clans, together with other criminals from Lazio, Veneto, and Liguria—two affiliates are intercepted laughing about recent Antimafia arrests in Holland. One of them says "*they really don't understand anything about the 'ndrangheta, really, they make their own stuff up!*",[6] mocking the attempts of foreign authorities to investigate different trafficking routes without grasping the real core of the issue at hand, the 'ndrangheta "*behaviour*".

Germany and Switzerland

The case studies of Germany and Switzerland are particularly illustrative for understanding the movements of the '*ndrine* in Europe. The National Antimafia Directorate (DNA 2012: 109) had already noticed how Germany and Switzerland have been destinations of the highest numbers of Calabrian immigrants (54,795 migrants towards Germany, 36,827 towards Switzerland). It is today common knowledge that there is 'ndrangheta presence in Germany, especially after the massacre of Duisburg on 15 August 2007, when six men were shot by a rival group in front of a restaurant. The event was linked to a feud in Calabria, in San Luca—the heart of the Aspromonte mountain in the Reggio Calabria hinterland. The Duisburg massacre revealed to the greater public not only the violence and reach of the 'ndrangheta abroad, but also the limits of international cooperation to fight the mafia (Europol 2013; Caneppele and Sarno 2013). The former Chief of Antimafia in Catanzaro still remembers the anger and frustration of that period[7]:

> We totally failed in Duisburg. It was the second time the 'ndrangheta had gone public, you know, with an event of public display, after the killing of Vice-President [of Calabrian Council] Fortugno in 2005, and we failed. We did nothing compared to what we could have done, we could not confiscate in Germany, we had to negotiate with Germany, we lost a precious opportunity.

After Duisburg, the question of penetration of the 'ndrangheta in Germany became of interest to the German authorities as well, under direction of the prosecutors in Konstanz. The main issue was the extent of the infiltration of the clans and their connection with Calabrian migrants. Sciarrone and Storti (2014) have already noticed how more than strategically moving to Germany, the clans have rather exploited the possibility to make effective use of the immigrant community. Furthermore, the geopolitical situation of Germany, its strategic position towards both Eastern Europe and Northern Europe, and the robustness of its economy were (and still are) all factors attracting the clans (Forgione 2008; Sciarrone and Storti 2014).

Operations Patriarca, Helvetia, and Rheinbrücke, among others, have recently investigated the activities of the clans between Germany and Switzerland confirming their settlement and indicating a colonisation model (DNA 2015, 2016). However, it is still Operation Crimine[8] the most relevant operation to understand the structure of the clans in this part of Europe. The links between the *locali* in Germany and Switzerland is confirmed by the affiliates themselves. In particular Mr Nesci, the Calabrian boss of the locale in Singen in Southern Germany, tightly linked to the clans in Rosarno in the west of Reggio Calabria, reveals how they have been under the Calabrian *Crimine* for seven years, how they *"cannot do anything without orders from down there"*,[9] how there would be violent repercussions if anyone tried.

Other *locali* are in Rielasingen, Radolfzell, Ravensburg, Engen, and Frankfurt in Germany, while clans in Switzerland (in Fravenfeld, in the canton of Thurgau) often tried to gain power in Germany as well. The structure of the *locali* is dependent on the clans in Calabria, through *infiltration* in the local economy and *settlement* in society (Sciarrone and Storti 2014). They adopted the same basic structural organisation (*'ndrina, locale*, minor and major *società*). The various operations in the past five years have shown how the dependence from Calabria relates to new affiliations, the ranking of the affiliates, the solution of controversies between the clans in Germany and those in Switzerland, general directives in criminal activities, and the development of vote-buying capability to build political influence in European elections (DNA 2016). Furthermore, the existence of these articulations in Germany and in Switzerland that follow the rules of their Calabrian partners, who are from very specific areas of Calabria (Rosarno, Fabrizia near Vibo Valentia, Reggio city, and Crotone), reinforces the structure of the clans in Calabria. The benefit is mutual: the clans in Germany have autonomy in their criminal endeavours, which benefits the clans in Calabria or in other parts of Italy in a tight net of contacts. At the same time, the German clans enjoy protection, mafia skills, and know-how from the clans in Calabria, access to contacts and money inside and outside Europe, and also the benefits of the mafia reputation that comes with the *'ndranghetisation* process, notwithstanding which part of Calabria the clans of origin are from.

WORLD MOVEMENTS BETWEEN GREED AND MIGRATION

Most of what we know about the presence and movements of the *'ndrine* in the rest of the world comes from Antimafia operations in Italy investigating drug trafficking networks pivoting around various 'ndrangheta clans. As we will see in Part II of this book, what emerges from investigations of the past years—especially from those highlighting the links between 'ndrangheta clans in Europe and those in South and North America—is the development of particular aggressive tactics by the Calabrian clans in their attempt to access the best drugs on the market and to increase their control of the drug trade in the main hotspots of Europe. As we leave to the next chapter the task of mapping the clans in the American continent in relation to the drug trade, here we need to clarify two points: first, the nature of the ethnic element in 'ndrangheta movements outside Europe, including the links with migration; and second, the opportunity-based decision-making also in the choices of destination and structures adopted abroad—what Sciarrone (2009) calls agency factors of mafia expansion.

We can apply some of the findings of the German situation and of the more general European presence of the clans also to the situation outside Europe. In Germany, the clans have infiltrated and then settled in *"territorial niches"* (Sciarrone and Storti 2014: 52); the exploitation of existing Calabrian communities in certain areas has made the initial *infiltration* (through the physical presence of mafia members on the spot) much easier, but their stationing, their successful *settlement*, has certainly happened also thanks to local conditions. It cannot be stressed enough that the "ethnic" dimension of the clans, their Calabrian origin, is just one of the factors of their success and it is more linked to shared socio-cultural behaviour that might or might not come with shared ethnicity (Christopher et al. 2014). It is not that Calabrians (or Sicilians or Campanian) migrants to Germany have carried mafia skills *tout court*. It seems more plausible that—when the need to invest and enter in certain convenient illegal sectors has arisen—the structure of the *'ndrine* in Calabria was strong enough and well equipped, in terms of money and human capital, to gain access also through the exploitation of ethnic brotherhood and the use of a consolidated *'ndranghetist behaviour*. Blood ties and Calabrian birth still are one of the reasons why the clans are successful abroad, but at the same time the ability of the clans to identify opportunities in existing and new illegal markets is indispensable. Both their structure, so deeply rooted to Calabria, and their business acumen in seizing profitable opportunities, therefore, allow for successful colonisation and settlement abroad.

On the other side, this does not mean that whenever criminal opportunities emerge abroad there will be an attempt to recreate and replicate the Calabrian criminal structure. In the case of the Netherlands, France, Spain, or the UK, for example, while we do have some indicators of a significant presence, the presence of the clans is fluid and does not congregate in cloned structures of the *'ndrine* in Calabria. Also, we do not know whether this depends on the type of illegal activities carried out in these areas, or on the ability of the *'ndrine* in Calabria to control other clans or affiliates in these countries directly from Calabria, or it is only blindness of the authorities so far. Certainly, if a smaller number of individuals linked to the clans are resident on a stable basis in certain territories, the clans might choose to keep contacts through increased travelling and movements of their own affiliates from Italy as needed, depending on the activity as well. This does not seem to be a very problematic choice given Europe's fast transport system today.

These considerations can also be applied to read certain situations outside of Europe. As we will see in Chap. 5, certain countries are origin or transit points for international traffics, which do necessitate a specific type of attention *in loco* by the 'ndrangheta clans. These are namely Peru, Colombia, Mexico, Brazil, and Morocco. Similarly, the USA, with its historical presence of mafia of Sicilian origin and with Calabrian individuals supporting Cosa Nostra (Critchley 2009), has in the past years attracted more 'ndrangheta members attempting to consolidate their reach in the US drug market. Two countries, Canada and Australia, do exhibit different traits, more similar to the German case, but also very different from it, considering their distance from Calabria, their migration routes, and the different occasions and opportunities the clans have (had) there. Not only Canada and Australia represent forms closer to a colonisation process with long-lasting settlements of clans of Calabrian origins, but the fate of these two countries has often been linked to one another across the globe; in the middle between them is always Calabria, where everything starts and everything ends.

Canada

Similarly to Germany, Canada has known the presence of criminals more or less linked to 'ndrangheta clans, affiliated to clans in Calabria and resident within Canadian borders, since the beginning of the last century (Nicaso 2005). After Argentina and Australia, and before the USA, Canada is the third country in the world in terms of number of Calabrian migrants (22,164 as processed by the AIRE in 2006 and reported by the DNA (2012: 109)). Next to other strong criminal organisations, among which a Canadian version of Cosa Nostra, outlaw motorcycle gangs, and narco-traffickers, the 'ndrangheta has rooted mostly in Ontario (Gratteri and Nicaso 2015; Nicaso and Lamothe 2005). *"Canada has always been"*—according to a prosecutor in Reggio[10]—*"the official 'transplantation place' of any clan who wanted to go abroad"*. Thanks to the possibility to activate cooperation through Calabrian migrants there, the links with Canada have existed since the clans needed them, probably since the kidnapping season, when the ransom money was also sent abroad for easier concealing (Nicaso and Lamothe 1995).

Also strong for their closeness to the USA, particularly New York, and with a mixed structure that sees both Calabrian and Sicilian affiliates, the 'ndrangheta clans in Canada today have a concrete possibility to participate in international drug trafficking in that part of the world, but they still engage in extortions to the Italian community, in selling counterfeit materials, and in illegal gambling, especially in the area of Woodbridge in Toronto (DNA 2012). This has been confirmed incessantly by Antimafia operations in the past ten years. However, alongside the role of the Canadian clans in the drug trade, the main operations involving Canada also confirm the importance of the Canadian clans for the structure and reputation of the '*ndrine* in Calabria. The clans in Canada, like those in Germany and to a lesser extent in Switzerland, are organic to the structure of the 'ndrangheta in Calabria, but still enjoy a high degree of autonomy. While the DNA (2016) has confirmed through Operation Bacinella 1 and 2 that there is a presence of clans from the area of Catanaro active in Canada, certainly historical investigations in the country relate to the village of Siderno, in the Reggio Calabria hinterland.

Operation Siderno Group[11] in Reggio Calabria established that since the 1950s, a coordination structure exists between Canada and Calabria (and Australia) among the clans from the area of Siderno in the province of Reggio Calabria. This coordination was originally wanted by Albert Anastasia and Frank Costello, members of Cosa Nostra in the USA and Calabrian of origin. The Siderno Group of Crime, especially active in Greater Toronto, soon became the reference point for Calabrian criminals in Canada and has often attempted to infiltrate local politics. This has been confirmed in Operation Crimine,[12] which proved how members of the Canadian clans visited Calabria to receive directives and advice on solutions to their problems while affiliates from Siderno participated in reunions in Toronto. The operation also proved that in Canada there is one of the two foreign "chambers of control" of the *Crimine* from Reggio Calabria, the other being in Australia. The judges agreed that there is not only a tight connection between Calabria (in the area of Reggio Calabria) and Canada, but also that the two structures depend on each other (DNA 2012). The existence of the *Canadian Crimine* means certainly the connection with the clans from the area of Reggio, via the *società* of Siderno. During an intercepted conversation in the laundry-mat owned by the boss Giuseppe Commisso in Siderno in 2009, a member of the *locale* of Thunder Bay (Ontario) lamented some misunderstandings with the society of the nine *locali* in Toronto. The boss suggested that this was a problem to be solved by the *Canadian Crimine*, as local articulation of the Calabrian one. The boss reminds the others: *"This is the rule, if there is any discipline at all... you are in the Crimine, not in a 'ndrina"*,[13] as a reminder of the difference between the unit structure and the collegial one.

In confirmation of this, local investigations in Siderno also demonstrate the organic participation of Canadian clans to the life of the *'ndrine* in Calabria and the commission of transnational crimes linked to mafia activities. Operation Falsa Politica[14] proved how certain politicians went to consult the boss Giuseppe Commisso in Siderno to ask for his blessing during the elections. In an intercepted conversation in 2010, the boss was upset about an affiliate from a nearby village who had dared to promote someone in Canada without prior approval by the *Crimine*. He said[15]:

> He is disrespecting everyone, in Canada, they are all from Siderno there... and he goes there and he gives the *dote* without saying a word! We try so hard here to respect each other and then he goes there...! I told him, you have to go and change the *copiata*[16] and do it all over again there or else, if you want us to be friends and to respect each other and to keep doing this. Otherwise, let's stop pretending and everyone stays in its *locale* and everything ends there. Things have to be done in the right way, the *copiata* has be the one from there, not because it is better, it's just... you cannot do what you want, not you, not me, no- one here can.

Australia

It is quite peculiar that, as it emerges from judicial documents, the fate of Australia appears to be so connected to that of Canada, again through the Siderno connection. Operation Siderno Group and Operation Crimine in fact have also revealed the links between the *'ndrine* in Calabria and their partners in certain areas of Australia. Similarly to Canada, in Australia, the presence of individuals linked to the Calabrian mafia dates back to the beginning of the last century and is incontrovertibly related to the migration of Calabrians to Australian states before and after the World Wars (Sergi 2015; Schneider 2009). Australia is the second recipient of Calabrian immigrants (23,580 as recorded by the AIRE and reported by the DNA (2012: 109); the bulk of migrants came from the Aspromonte area and the Reggio Calabria hinterland. Australia is an example of colonisation: there are both an historical settlement of Calabrian criminals organised locally since the 1950s throughout the 1980s and a rekindling of illegal activities in connection with Calabrian clans since the 2000s (Sergi 2012, 2016).

Even though Australian authorities already knew the Calabrian 'ndrangheta in the 1960s, the knowledge of the clans in Australia, their connection with one another on the territory, and the extent of their infiltration in public affairs and legal economy is under-researched (Bennetts 2016; Sergi 2015, 2016). After a large ecstasy bust in 2008 in Melbourne, organised by Calabrian clans in Victoria, and following a political scandal in 2005 which related to the visa of a Calabrian citizen again in Melbourne (then convicted for drug importation as member of the 'ndrangheta in the ecstasy bust of 2008), media attention to the phenomenon of the Calabrian mafia has been escalating (Small and Gilling 2016). Political connections and involvement in large importations of drugs in the country appear to be the two characteristics of the mafia in Australia (McKenzie et al. 2015). Also, in Australia, findings in the anthropological literature about Calabrian migration point at the preservation of Calabrian rituals, relationships, and alliances among families (Marino and Chiro 2014), which are consistent with mafia settlements (Bennetts 2016). Two codes of affiliation have been found in Australia and visits of Italian law enforcement agents to Australia have confirmed the existence of structured *'ndrine* and *locali*, on the model of their Calabrian counterparts and still connected to Calabria through family ties (Macrì and Ciconte 2009).

In Antimafia judicial documents, however, Australian connections look more scattered than the ones of Germany and Canada or the rest of Italy. Certainly, the presence of units parallel in structure to those in Calabria has been object of judicial attention since investigations during Operation Olimpia,[17] which established that Australia (in particular, Griffith in New South Wales) had been the destination of some of the ransom money from the kidnappings (Spagnolo 2010; Macrì and Ciconte 2009; Forgione 2008) and that the clans in Griffith had also murdered those who might stand in the way of their wealth invested in cannabis plantations (Small and Gilling 2009; Sergi 2015).

Operation Crimine, again, provided new evidence of Australian–Calabrian connections. In Australia, there is an articulation of the *Crimine* of Reggio Calabria, which indicates the presence of various clans in the country. This emerged from the visit in Siderno of an Australian–Calabrian individual—someone also holding a political role in Australia—who asked to the boss Commisso permission and approval to lead his own *locale* in Stirling, near Perth, while also giving details on other clans across Australia. It is always through interceptions in Siderno of the boss Commisso that we learn about the existence of a structure in Australia that handles Australian issues among local clans—the *Australian Crimine*—and that, according to the magistrates, also dates back to 1960s (Sergi 2015; Macrì and Ciconte 2009). Commisso, as in the Canadian case, is very weary of the rules of solving any issue in Australia first[18]:

> If you are not good there, you are not good here either. If you have issues you have to solve them there, among yourselves, if you come here and you have had problems there and you have not solved them there, we cannot do anything.

According to an Antimafia prosecutor in Reggio Calabria, out of the findings during and after Operation *Crimine*, not only it is clear that there is a Little Italy of Calabrian origin in certain areas of Australia (Melbourne, New South Wales and especially Sydney and Griffith, Adelaide, and Perth) but certainly *"they keep in touch, they travel a lot, ours [Calabrians] go there as Australians come here, it is handled in person whenever they can"*.[19] According to the Federal Police in Australia, today's presence of the 'ndrangheta is certainly not limited to the historical links in New South Wales, Perth, Melbourne, or Adelaide, but it has mutated and re-activated the links with the new generations of Calabrian descendants in Australia (McKenzie et al. 2015).

CONCLUSION

The cases presented in this chapter, especially those of colonisation—more interesting under the profile of the structure of the 'ndrangheta today—have more than one thing in common. Obviously, there are the links with the Calabrian community, which, however, should be understood and not demonised. We would not go as far as saying that *"migration is unlikely to be a decisive factor"* (Calderoni et al. 2015: 15) for the movements and settlements of the 'ndrangheta abroad. Even if it is at times true that *"the emergence of the mafias has often occurred at times different from those of the main migratory flows"* (Sciarrone and Storti 2014: 53), the links with the Calabrian community certainly weight differently abroad, especially in the farthest countries, than they do in Italy. In some cases, like Australia for example, the existence of migrants might indeed determine the reason for the *continuation* of activities, beyond the initial settlements. Certainly, the connections between new generations and old clans need to be further explored. There is nothing inherently criminal in Calabrian migration; there is however, the possibility to exploit and re-activate family links through migration from clans that bask in their criminal reputation. The 'ndrangheta abroad—in Germany, Canada, and Australia—tends to adopt the same set of behaviours to secure the *'ndranghetisation* process; it attempts control of territories or portions of territory and it attempts to ingratiate political spheres through cultivation of relationships with local communities usually via Calabrian communities. There are various factors that might influence different contexts and outcomes. Colonisation phenomena outside of Italy have been possible because (a) someone, in Calabria, with enough charisma has managed to create and sustain a unitary structure and become a reference point also for people in other countries; and (b) the set of rituals, rules, traditions, and values of the criminal organisation were rooted and have persisted in some individuals or groups in the country of destination or remain appealing there also today. Also, the exploitation of certain areas is part of current needs and opportunity-based choices of the Calabrian clans, as demonstrated by the preservation and rekindling of relationships abroad and the reliance upon foreign "chambers of control".

In conclusion, when the 'ndrangheta moves, it is both static and dynamic. It is *dynamic* because through delocalised activities and colonisation patterns it manages to move quickly and effectively within illegal markets. It is, however, also *static,* because the core of the delocalised activities, as well as the "original sin" of colonisation, remains anchored, steadily, to Calabria. In other words, the *dynamism* of the clans would not be sustainable without their *stasis* in Calabria. The existence of such a fractured reality in Calabria—ensuring *dynamism* and allowing the variety of movements of individual clans—and the shared *'ndranghetist* set of behaviour—preserving the *stasis* and allowing to maintain a certain unity among autonomous structures—are the ingredients of successful mafia movements and *'ndranghetisation* of existing clans abroad.

NOTES

1. Operation Crimine, No. 1389/2008 R.G.N.R. DDA.
2. Investigative Antimafia Directorate (DIA), I Rep., No.125/I/IIIDiv/H14, Prot. 020464 Roma 17.05.2011.
3. Operation Mauser, No. 3427/06 R.G. GIP.
4. Operation Acero, No. 7428/2010 R.G.N.R. DDA.
5. Operation Krupy, No. 57055/12 R.G.N.R. DDA .
6. Operation Krupy, No. 57055/12 R.G.N.R. DDA, p. 65.
7. Interview in Catanzaro, DDA Procura della Repubblica, 05 January 2014, translated from Italian.

8. Operation Crimine, No. 1389/2008 R.G.N.R. DDA.
9. Operation Crimine, No. 1389/2008 R.G.N.R. DDA, p. 144.
10. Interview in Reggio Calabria, DDA Procura della Repubblica, 16 December 2015, translated from Italian.
11. Operation Siderno Group No. 24/92 R.G.N.R. DDA.
12. Operation Crimine, No. 1389/2008 R.G.N.R. DDA.
13. Operation Crimine, No. 1389/2008 R.G.N.R. DDA, sentence GUP 2010, p. 198.
14. Operation Falsa Politica, No.7144/2011 R.G.N.R. DDA + No. 4607/2011 R.G. GIP.
15. Operation Falsa Politica, No.7144/2011 R.G.N.R. DDA + No. 4607/2011 R.G. GIP, pp. 717–718.
16. The "*copiata*" is the set of three names that every new affiliate of a superior ranking needs to remember as the three people, higher in ranking, who gave him the new charge.
17. Operation Olimpia, No. 104/95 R.G.N.R. DDA.
18. Operation Crimine, No. 1389/2008 R.G.N.R. DDA, sentence GUP 2010, p. 200.
19. Interview in Reggio Calabria, DDA Procura della Repubblica, 04 April 2015, translated from Italian.

REFERENCES

Allum, F. (2013). Italian Organised Crime in the UK. *Policing, 6*(4), 354–359.

Arsovska J. (2015). Strategic Mobsters or Deprived Migrants? Testing the Transplantation and Deprivation Models of Organized Crime in an Effort to Understand Criminal Mobility and Diversity in the United States. *International Migration* Online First, (DOI: 10.1111/imig.12217).

Bennetts S. (2016). Undesirable Italians: Prolegomena for a history of the Calabrian 'Ndrangheta in Australia. *Modern Italy*. doi:10.1017/mit.2015.5.

Campana P. (2013). Understanding then Responding to Italian Organized Crime Operations across Territories. *Policing*. DOI: 10.1093/police/pat012.

Christopher, J. C., Wendt, D. C., Marecek, J., et al. (2014). Critical Cultural Awareness: Contributions to a Globalizing Psychology. *The American psychologist, 69*(7), 645–655.

Bernardotti, A. (2015). Direzione America del Sud. Le nuove migrazioni italiane in Argentina. In: Gjergji, I. (ed.), *La nuova emigrazione italiana. Cause, mete e figure sociali*. Venezia: Edizioni Ca' Foscari.

Calderoni, F., Berlusconi, G., Garofalo, L., et al. (2015). The Italian mafias in the world: A systematic assessment of the mobility of criminal groups. *European Journal of Criminology*. DOI: 10.1177/1477370815623570

Caneppele, S., & Sarno, F. (2013). La presenza internazionale della'Ndrangheta secondo le recenti indagini. *Sicurezza e scienze sociali, 3*, 161–176.

Cingari, G. (1982). *Storia della Calabria dall'Unità a Oggi*. Bari: Editori Laterza.

Critchley, D. (2009). *The origin of organized crime in America: the New York City mafia, 1891–1931*. London: Routledge.

Del Boca, D. & Venturini, A. (2003). Italian migration. *IZA Discussion paper series* 938.

DNA. (2012). *Relazione annuale sulle attività svolte dal Procuratore Nazionale Antimafia e dalla Direzione Nazionale Antimafia nonché sulle dinamiche e strategie della criminalità organizzata di tipo mafioso*. Roma: Direzione Nazionale Antimafia.

DNA. (2014). *Relazione annuale sulle attività svolte dal Procuratore Nazionale Antimafia e dalla Direzione Nazionale Antimafia nonché sulle dinamiche e strategie della criminalità organizzata di tipo mafioso*. Roma: Direzione Nazionale Antimafia.

DNA. (2015). *Relazione annuale sulle attività svolte dal Procuratore Nazionale Antimafia e dalla Direzione Nazionale Antimafia nonché sulle dinamiche e strategie della criminalità organizzata di tipo mafioso*. Roma: Direzione Nazionale Antimafia.

DNA. (2016). *Relazione annuale sulle attività svolte dal Procuratore nazionale e dalla Direzione nazionale antimafia e antiterrorismo nonché sulle dinamiche e strategie della criminalità organizzata di tipo mafioso*. Roma: Direzione Nazionale Antimafia e Antiterrorismo.

Europol. (2013). *Threat Assessment Italian Organised Crime*. The Hague: Europol.

Fondazione Migrantes. (2014). *Rapporto Italiani nel Mondo*. Todi: Tav Editrice.

Forgione, F. (2008). *Relazione Annuale sulla 'Ndrangheta*. Roma: Commissione Parlamentare d'inchiesta sul fenomeno della mafia e sulle altre associazioni criminali.

Franzina, E. (1998). *La storia altrove: casi nazionali e casi regionali nelle moderne migrazioni di massa*. Cierre: Verona.

Gratteri, N., & Nicaso, A. (2015). *Oro bianco*. Milan: Mondadori.

ISTAT. (2007a). Espatri e rimpatri per regione e ripartizione geografica—Anni 1876–2005. *Serie Storiche. L'archivio della statistica Italiana*. Roma: ISTAT—Istituto Nazionale di Statistica.

ISTAT. (2007b). Espatriati per alcuni Paesi di destinazione—Anni 1869–2005. *Serie Storiche. L'archivio della statistica Italiana*. Roma: ISTAT—Istituto Nazionale di Statistica.

ISTAT. (2014) International and internal migration. *Socio-demographic and environmental statistics directorate*. Rome: ISTAT—Italian National Institute of Statistics.

Macrì, V., & Ciconte, E. (2009). *Australian 'Ndrangheta*. Soveria Mannelli: Rubbetino.

Marino, S., & Chiro, G. (2014). Family alliances and Comparatico among a group of Calabrian-Australian families living in Adelaide, South Australia. *Journal of Anthropological Research, 70*, 107–130.

McKenzie, N., Hichens, C., and Toft, K. (2015). Part One: The Mafia in Australia: Drugs, Murder and Politics. Part Two: The Mafia in Australia: Blood Ties. *ABC Four Corners and Fairfax Media*. http://www.abc.net.au/4corners/stories/2015/06/29/4261876.htm

Ministero degli Affari Esteri. (2005). *La rilevazione degli italiani all'estero al 21 marzo 2003: caratteristiche demografiche*. Roma: ISTAT.

Nicaso, A. (2005). *Rocco Perri: The story of Canada's most notorious bootlegger*. Canada: John Wiley & Sons.

Nicaso, A., & Lamothe, L. (1995). *Global mafia: The new world order of organized crime*. Toronto: Macmillan Canada.

Nicaso, A., & Lamothe, L. (2005). *Angels, mobsters & narco-terrorists: The rising menace of global criminal empires*. Mississauga, Ont.: John Wiley & Sons Canada.

O'Reilly, K. (2007). Intra-European migration and the mobility—enclosure dialectic. *Sociology, 41*(2), 277–293.

Schneider, S. (2009). *Iced: The story of organized crime in Canada*. Mississauga, Ont.: J. Wiley and Sons Canada.

Sciarrone, R. (2009). *Mafie vecchie, mafie nuove : Radicamento ed espansione*. Roma: Donzelli.

Sciarrone, R., & Storti, L. (2014). The territorial expansion of mafia-type organized crime. The case of the Italian mafia in Germany. *Crime, Law and Social Change, 61*(1), 37–60.

Sergi, A. (2012). Family Influence: Italian mafia group operates in Australia. *Jane's Intelligence Review* (August): 46–47.

Sergi, A. (2013). La 'ndrangheta migrante e il caso Australia. In V. Cappelli, G. Masi, & P. Sergi (Eds.), *Calabria migrante*. Centro di Ricerca sulle Migrazioni: Rende.

Sergi, A. (2015). The evolution of the Australian 'ndrangheta. An historical perspective. *Australian & New Zealand Journal of Criminology, 48*(2), 155–174.

Sergi, A. (2016). Countering the Australian 'Ndrangheta. The criminalisation of mafia behaviour in Australia between national and comparative criminal law. *Australian & New Zealand Journal of Criminology* (in press).

Small, C., & Gilling, T. (2009). *Smack express. Organised crime got hooked on drugs*. Allen & Unwin: Crows Nest.

Small, C., & Gilling, T. (2016). *Evil Life: The True Story of the Calabrian Mafia in Australia*. Sydney: Allen & Unwin.

Spagnolo, P. (2010). L'ascesa della 'ndrangheta in Australia. *Altreitalie*, January–June.

Varese, F. (2011). *Mafias on the move: how organized crime conquers new territories*, Princeton, NJ, Oxford: Princeton University Press.

PART II

Illegal Activities

CHAPTER 5

Drug Trafficking and Investments

Abstract This chapter looks at the main revenue of the 'ndrangheta—that is, drug trafficking. It describes the main judicial operations that have tracked the presence of 'ndrangheta members and brokers around the world. After describing the way the clans have entered drug markets since the 1970s, the focus shall be on the most contemporary Antimafia investigations. These investigations are crucial to understand not only the changing structure of the clans, but also their reach. This chapter will argue that the drug trade is profoundly linked to the control of the territory in Calabria and in particular of the port of Gioia Tauro. Finally, this chapter will look at the management of proceeds of crime by the clans, especially focusing on investigations on money laundering.

Keywords Drug Trade • Cocaine • Port of Gioia Tauro • Criminal Reputation • Money Laundering

INTRODUCTION

Drug trafficking has been considered for years the main revenue of 'ndrangheta clans. According to the National Antimafia Directorate, *"through the Port of Gioia Tauro goes at least half of the cocaine imported to Italy"* (DNA 2014: 128). The DNA (2016: 39) has confirmed that in the past three years over 3 tons of cocaine have been seized in the Port of Gioia Tauro. Cocaine, says the Antimafia Directorate (DNA 2016), is transported in

© The Editor(s) (if applicable) and The Author(s) 2016
A. Sergi, A. Lavorgna, *'Ndrangheta*,
DOI 10.1007/978-3-319-32585-9_5

various ways, such as inside eggs swallowed by humans or animals or in vacuum-sealed packages inside elastic bands carried by couriers, in belts that can carry up to 1.5 kg of drug, or in liquid forms in fake whiskey bottles. The increasing attention by law enforcement agencies over the port of Gioia Tauro—where drugs arrive in containers from at least three different routes across the Atlantic and from Africa (Sergi 2015)—has followed the past years' attempts to understand how the territory around Gioia Tauro is governed by local mafia clans and their allies. The clans involvement in drug trafficking is obviously motivated by the huge amount of money. Between July 2013 and July 2014 alone, in Gioia Tauro the fiscal police (*Guardia di Finanza*) seized 1,406,065 kg of cocaine; it is estimated that in that period 1 kg of cocaine was bought for roughly 4000 euros to the producers while the retail price can be multiplied up to ten times (DNA 2015: 19). By following recent Antimafia operations, and while reading intercepted conversations and witnesses' statements, we can observe the flexibility of 'ndrangheta members in their roles as drug traffickers and their ability to adapt and change their strategies very quickly.

Linked to the drug trade is also the necessity to launder the proceeds of crime, thus the financial operations of the clans also need to be considered in this chapter. As it would be impossible in such a short volume to put together a comprehensive analysis of everything that has emerged in the past years in relation to drug trade and 'ndrangheta clans, this chapter will focus on the description and analysis of the most salient Antimafia operations, as also discussed in interviews with magistrates in Calabria, to explain the main reasons behind the clans' successes over the past years.

Entering and Dominating the Drug Trade

As said in Chap. 2, the turning point in history for the 'ndrangheta clans, considering also the economic status of the Calabrian region, is in between the 1970s and the 1980s. In that period, most clans acquired the necessary power and wealth to enter the drug trade at the national and international level, challenging and overcoming—or at least competing with—their Sicilian neighbours. Calabria at that time was facing more than one issue in terms of its own political status, with the new regional settlement,[1] and with a number of interventions that in the 1960s were aiming at changing the economy of the region. To the instability of the regional governance—unable to meet the challenges of a territory geographically demanding and diverse, and of a process for industrialisation always promised and never delivered by the central state—was paired a mafia power, which was getting stronger and stronger (Cingari 1982). By the end of the 1980s, some of the clans, already active especially around the Aspromonte area, started accumulating money through kidnappings by exploiting their knowledge of the territory and by investing the money from cigarette smuggling. As already underlined, this made them notorious throughout the country (Sergi 1991). The money accumulated from ransoms was then invested into fruitful cooperation with Sicilian Cosa Nostra to enter the drug trade. However, as Cosa Nostra, Camorra groups, and the Sacra Corona Unita were in those years maimed by Antimafia actions, the Calabrian clans managed to establish themselves as the most credible, reliable, and stable partners for drug trafficking groups outside of Italy (Forgione 2008).

One of the first books on the 'ndrangheta written by Sharo Gambino in 1975 declares how it was *"almost certain"* that Crotone was the epicentre of the drug trade; it was the first place where police and local authorities had started to notice strange movements and had later discovered drug couriers for Cosa Nostra (Gambino 1975: 140). During 1986 and 1988, Operation Pizza Connection 2 (Sergi 1988)—also known as Operation Calabria Connection (Sergi 1991: 102)—found that in Calabria heroin and cocaine were exchanged out of agreements between Cosa Nostra in Palermo and allies in New York. Calabrian brokers, already at that time, were travelling from Calabria to New York and based their affairs in the area of Reggio Calabria and Crotone. Operation Pizza Connection 2 indicated that there might have been a link between the violent mafia feuds happening in those years in Calabria and the adjustments over the drug trade in the region. This finds confirmation in the trials for Operation Olimpia,[2] which started in the mid-1990s and ended in 2001. At that time, the clans had already established their roles in the drug business and were already cementing their alliances to avoid wasting money, time, and men in mafia feuds.

Subsequently, all the three Operations Decollo (I, II, III) between 2000 and 2011, followed '*ndranghetisti* around the world, with investigations that touched four different continents, from Australia to Canada, from the USA to African countries. These ten-year-long investigations represent the first window into the positions and the relevance of 'ndrangheta clans into the contemporary global drug trade. Operations Decollo I,[3] in particular, after almost a decade of investigations gave for the first time the dimension of the drug trade to/from and through Calabrian clans. As we read in the court order,[4] one of the crucial finding of the investigation was the understanding of the way the clans (in this case predominantly the '*ndrine* from the Vibo Valentia area) dealt with traffickers in Latin America on a rolling basis. Trust had been established throughout the years; the clans bought specific amounts of drugs from the same sellers in Mexico on a permanent basis. The relationship, say the Antimafia prosecutors in Catanzaro, was and still is stable and continuous and is fortified by the "good" reputation of reliability of the Calabrian clans among drug sellers.

In the documents of all three Operations Decollo, we also read about the relationship existing internally, in Calabria, among the various clans, the destination of the drugs (mainly Milano, in the north of Italy), and the role of brokers, who are able to intersect and mediate the interests between buyers and sellers directly in Venezuela, Bolivia, Peru, Mexico, and Colombia. Next to the brokers, Operations Decollo also revealed a complex network of political supporters of the clans, which is perfectly in line with the sociological analysis of the 'ndrangheta power as addressed in the previous sections of this book. In the interceptions during Operation Decollo, we can also find indications of how the clans operate and how they practically divide and distribute the drugs. The clans' organisational structure allows them to effectively face various crisis of shortage of cocaine for their various dealers in Milano, which also highlight the stability of the brand name and the tight contact among the various clans, the producers, and the sellers. One dealer is intercepted begging to "*fix the problem*" as he "*feels like crying*" but he is reassured by a clan member that someone will intervene as a guarantor to solve the issue, "*as usual*".[5] In fact, most clans are able to control the way the drug is distributed once it arrives (also after a shortage crisis) depending on the agreed methods of payment and the smoothness of the trafficking mechanisms.

Between 1970s and 2010, the clans have consolidated their roles in the drug trade on two levels. First level is *internal*: the clans have learned how to cooperate among themselves, in terms of drug importations, risk sharing, and crisis management. The second level is *external*: the wealthiest clans in terms of money and men power (including access to brokers and facilitators) are able to import large quantities of drugs directly from the producer countries thanks to their connections with other organised crime groups across Europe as well. This successful internal and external collaboration has progressively allowed for the acquisition and consolidation of the roles of various clans in the drug trade both at the importation and at the distribution stage, as well as the solidification of significant power to influence their partners around the world.

THE LATEST INTERNATIONAL INVESTIGATIONS INTO THE DRUG TRADE

According to the Antimafia National and District Directorates in Catanzaro and Reggio Calabria, the 'ndrangheta clans know no rivals today in Italy and abroad when it comes to drug trafficking. This claim, which sometimes provokes justifiable doubts and concerns among researchers and journalist in Italy and abroad (Calderoni 2012), has been repeated in every Antimafia reports since at least 2009. Not only the prosecutors assert a real hegemony of the Calabrian clans over cocaine trafficking from Latin America to Europe but they also argue how this almost monopolistic position in the drug trade has made the 'ndrangheta the only significant financial subject in Calabria (DNA 2015, 2016). The National Antimafia Directorate confidently declares that other criminal organisations refer to the 'ndrangheta clans to buy cocaine, making Calabrian clans the most reputable wholesaler in Italy and in Europe (DNA 2015: 14). As confirmed in one of the interviews in the Antimafia District Prosecution office in Reggio Calabria[6]:

> If it is not a monopoly, it certainly is an oligarchy. As we often say, if there were the seven sisters[7] in the cocaine trafficking network, like in the oil economic circuit, then the 'ndrangheta would definitely be one of the big sisters.

By looking into details at the most recent investigations, it seems certainly difficult to negate the hegemony claim so dear to prosecutors. It is indeed more than just a "negative pride" on the side of prosecutors talking about their job (Sergi 2016).

However, three main operations between 2014 and 2015 from Antimafia prosecutors in Reggio Calabria—Operation New Bridge, Operation Buongustaio, and Operations Columbus I and II, all involving international law enforcement partners—have highlighted in an unprecedented way not only the routes of cocaine and the degree of 'ndrangheta clans' involvement, but also the sophisticated sensibility of Calabrian prosecutors to the understanding of the phenomenon in its evolution.

Operation New Bridge

On 11 February 2014, Operation New Bridge[8] led to the arrest of 26 people for membership of an unlawful association finalised to cross-border drug trafficking, money laundering, and mafia association charges. Eighteen arrests were carried out by the Italian authorities in Calabria, and eight arrests by the FBI and the US Department of Justice in New York City (NYC). In the documents related to Operation New Bridge in both countries, the most significant element is the clarification of the relationship between members of the Gambino mafia family in NYC and the 'ndrangheta members belonging to the clans Ursino and Simonetta, from the East coast of the Reggio Calabria province. The trafficking of both heroin (around 1300 kg) and cocaine (over 500 kg) from Latin America to Calabria was organised through US-based intermediaries and interjected in various places in Italy and abroad (Senato della Repubblica 2015). Antimafia investigators have highlighted how Operation New Bridge represents a turning point for investigators: it shows how Sicilian mafia families, like the Gambino family, are now working together with the Calabrian clans rather than with Cosa Nostra ones, confirming once again the contemporary supremacy of the 'ndrangheta's brand and the successful 'ndranghetisation of the clans abroad.

When looking at the indictments and the coordinated efforts both in Calabria and in NYC to understand how the drug network worked, we observe not only established links between the two continents but also the pre-existence of such links to this operation. The FBI and the US Eastern District Attorney charged defendants based in NYC, mainly in Brooklyn: these individuals are Calabrians and with tight links to their Calabrian families. In addition to their origin and their affiliation to Calabrian clans in the motherland, this operation also revealed connections between these NY-based drug traffickers and Mexican drug cartels operating in Guyana who were supposed to send the drugs in shipments of frozen food. These shipments, some of which intercepted in Malaysia for a value of more than seven million US dollars, had been organised by the families in New York but were then supposed to arrive into the port of Gioia Tauro, which, the FBI wiretaps revealed, *"would guarantee the safe arrival of container ships containing contraband"* (FBI 2014).

Operation Buongustaio

Between August 2012 and August 2013, more than 500 kg of cocaine were seized in Italy (Gioia Tauro), Belgium (Antwerp), Spain (Valencia), Brazil (Saõ Paulo), and Portugal (Leixos). In March 2014, around 1500 kg of cocaine have been seized in various other locations in Italy, in the Netherlands, in Peru, in Montenegro, and in Serbia (DNA 2015).

All these seizures were part of Operation Buongustaio[9] directed by the prosecutors in Reggio Calabria together with the Brazilian Federal Police in Saõ Paulo, for a total of 44 people arrested and charged with mafia membership and international drug trafficking (Senato della Repubblica 2015). While arrests were executed simultaneously in Brazil and in Italy, the seizures involved Interpol and attachés of Brazilian police forces in England, Italy, and Spain (Campos 2014).

Operations Buongustaio had the great merit to uncover the functioning and the routes of drugs obtained from Peru and Bolivia, smuggled into Brazil via the port of Santos, and then sent to various destinations in Europe. From the combined reading of both the Italian and the Brazilian documents, it appears quite clearly how the drug importations had been a synergic effort of the Rivera-Pereira group in Saõ Paulo, the Radoman group in Holland, and the 'ndrangheta clan Ietto-Cua-Pipicella from the Aspromonte area near Reggio Calabria, with affiliates in Piemonte as well. The 'ndrangheta clans were the main investors in buying cocaine, and they were organising the shipments from Peru and Bolivia to Brazil. The majority of the European shipments, among those seized, had as final destination the Calabrian port of Gioia Tauro.

Operation Buongustaio represents not only a great example of international cooperation but also confirms the complex links between 'ndrangheta clans and groups in Brazil as well as between 'ndrangheta clans and other groups in Europe. Italian prosecutors during these operations noted how the Calabrian clans acted both as investors and as wholesalers or distributors. The flexibility in the roles performed demonstrates once again the adaptability to the risks and the responsiveness to the sudden changes of the drug markets.

Operations Columbus

On 7 May 2015, authorities in Reggio Calabria and in New York arrested 13 people in Queens, NYC. On 15 October 2015, other seven people were arrested in Costa Rica (DNA 2016). The two operations, known as Columbus I[10] and II,[11] have been targeting a drug trafficking network across Costa Rica, New York, and Calabria, with drug seizures also in Delaware and in Pennsylvania. The FBI in NYC and the Antimafia prosecutors in Reggio Calabria, together with authorities in Costa Rica, confirmed the existence of a network importing drugs, especially cocaine, based in Calabria and in New York and operating across the world, mainly in Europe.

Operations Columbus I and II represent the direct continuation of Operations Solares II,[12] which revealed an international drug ring scheme run in partnerships between the Schirripa family clan in NYC and in the East coast in the province of Reggio Calabria, and the Gulf Cartel in Mexico. Operations Solares and Columbus have in common not only the Latin America/North America/Calabria axis, but also the involvement in the investigations of *brokers* directly operating to ease off the partnerships with the Mexican groups. Since 2008, together with the Schirripa clan, the NY-based brokers had sought protection and support from the Cosa Nostra Genovese clan in NYC and to a lesser extent from the Lucchese and Gambino families too. Gregorio Gigliotti, the owner of an Italian restaurant in Queens, together with *'ndranghetisti* from clans in Siderno, Sinopoli, and Taurianova (near Reggio Calabria), had been considered as the main broker of several cocaine importations between the USA and Italy through shipments of fresh fruits and dairies organised through fictitious import–export companies intercepted in various European ports.

Operations Columbus I and II have confirmed the crucial role of brokers for the Calabrian clans in Mexico, Costa Rica, Bolivia, and Peru as well as the existence of a family-run business model at the core of the network: together with Gregorio Gigliotti, in fact, the authorities in NYC have arrested his sons and wife. Authorities have also focused on the language and the communication techniques behind these international trafficking, which include travels between Calabria and the USA and the USA and Costa Rica and, obviously, encrypted phone conversations in code with talks about food and even about paintings to deceive the listener. More importantly, Operations Columbus reconfirmed the existence of rolling contracts for the supply of cocaine between Latin America and Calabrian clans, already discovered during Operations Decollo. In these contracts, the 'ndrangheta brokers are virtually always in possession of the drugs and therefore able to instantly resell before a furniture order is actually even made.

THE PORT OF GIOIA TAURO: DRUG IMPORTATION AND DISTRIBUTION

From a careful reading of the latest investigations, it emerges that at the core of the 'ndrangheta reputation as an international drug importer and distributor is the port of Gioia Tauro. At least until now, the clans have used the port of Gioia Tauro as their cove, their harbour, and their shield.

The port of Gioia Tauro, as said in Chap. 2, is the perfect example of a project that since the beginning attracted mafia bosses who dreamed to exploit its potential. This potential today is, arguably, fully realised if we look at the high number of drug seizures (DNA 2016).

Until 2015, Antimafia prosecutors have been declaring quite strongly and quite consistently that, when it comes to drugs, Gioia Tauro has a unique and predominant role. Run through a cartel, Gioia Tauro has been *the* 'ndrangheta port. According to many Antimafia operations and trials during the 1990s and the 2000s, and lately reminded by Operation All Inside,[13] the port is run by a consortium of three local '*ndrine* (Piromalli-Molé, Bellocco, and Pesce). These families control the arrival of containers in the port, fix the prices to use the port, and handle the drugs—cocaine and heroin mainly—inside the containers by moving them via trucks to the rest of the region or to the rest of the country.

It is very important to understand the geography of the clans and the political and economic history of Gioia Tauro in order to understand the management of the port today. Intercepted materials throughout various investigations have confirmed that while the families from the areas of Vibo Valentia and West of Reggio Calabria maintain the direct control of Gioia Tauro, the families from the East areas of Reggio and from the area of Catanzaro and Crotone also use the port by trusting their allies with their importations while sharing the risks of seizure.

According to prosecutors in Reggio Calabria, there are at least three established routes from Gioia Tauro, which are recurrently exploited by mafia clans (Gratteri and Nicaso 2015; Sergi 2015). The first one is the "California Express" route: shipments from Northern America arrive in Panama through California and Mexico; from Panama, they collect smaller cargos arriving from Chile, Peru, Colombia, and Northern Brazil before leaving towards Gioia Tauro. The second route is known as "Medusa", with shipments that cruise the ports in the Gulf of Mexico before stopping in the Bahamas, where they collect containers arriving from South America, and then leave towards Gioia Tauro with a previous stop in Valencia, Spain. Shipments on the third route, instead, leave from Argentina towards Montevideo and Southern Brazil before leaving for Gioia Tauro.

The most observed and efficient system used to traffic drugs through these routes is the system of "rip-off" (Sergi 2015): neither the sender nor the receiver company knows about the cocaine in the containers. The clans arrange for someone they trust in the various ports to place the drugs in the various shipments; considering the amount of shipments arriving every day at Gioia Tauro, most of which in small cargos headed towards Northern Europe, it would be virtually impossible to check them all. Moreover, the "rip-off" system makes it very hard to prove ownership of the cargo while letting the drugs travel without any extra costs, such as, for example, corruption of couriers.

Transcripts of witnesses' statements collected during Operation All Inside have revealed simple and yet effective techniques to manage the drugs once in Gioia Tauro. In particular, during a hearing with the prosecutors, one witness said[14]:

> We always discussed about cocaine and heroin [at dinner with that group of people]. Heroin and cocaine arrive at the port of Gioia Tauro, then they move it through trucks and they divide it in various portions, here in town, in Rosarno. These are the big names, the Pesces with Rao, Leotta, De Marte… so they divide the portions here, but they want the money straight away, they are the big fish and they do all the work. There are others, like the Cacciolas, who used to get the drugs from people from the Ionic [East] coast, and now they come here too.

In Operation Buongustaio,[15] prosecutors confirmed how the port had been rented out to other criminal organisations in Italy and abroad, as it is considered secure enough to minimise the risks of trafficking. Other ports in the rest of Italy, like Venezia or Livorno or Genova, might be used as secondary harbours when Gioia Tauro is not immediately available. Interviews with prosecutors in Catanzaro, however, warn how the increasing focus on Gioia Tauro might eventually divert the clans' activities more towards other smaller ports in the region or other ports in Italy.

It is fundamental to notice that the peculiarity of Gioia Tauro does not lie only in its strategic geographical position. Certainly, the conditions of birth and evolution of the port are cause and effect of the primacy of local clans in drug trafficking networks. However, it is the ability to control those who work at the port—both new and old hires—that makes the difference in the governance of drugs in Gioia Tauro. Operation All Inside,[16] for example, showed the involvement of employees of the Medcenter Container Terminal S.p.A. in Gioia Tauro, who were caught collecting cocaine and transporting it outside the port area through trucks owned by the clans. It is not only through corruption and collusion that workers at the port of Gioia Tauro are representative of the "control of the territory" typical of mafia power. As perfectly put by the DNA (2015: 20)—and backed up by data on unemployment rates in Calabria (Banca d'Italia 2015)—*"it is not only a criminal choice [...]; it is about simple gratitude towards those who are the real reason for getting the job"*. As demonstrated by Operation All Inside[17] among others, in order to be hired to work at the port, the Pesce family and their associates had to be consulted directly, without mediation from other clans. This is how the local *'ndrine* have secured the hegemony over the routes of drugs through Gioia Tauro, together with the control—through extortion rackets or ownership and participation—of the import–export companies operating in the port.

MONEY LAUNDERING AND INVESTMENTS

The Financial Intelligence Unit within the Banca d'Italia estimated that around 99 % of the reported suspicious activities are cases of money laundering, for a total value of 164 billion euros only in 2014 (UIF 2015: 27). This extremely high figure mirrors a similar warning coming from SOS Impresa in 2012 (SOS Impresa 2012) that indicated 140 billion euros as annual estimate of money laundering. Apart from criticisms to these figures and their opaque methodologies, it is relevant to note that in the past years the Bank of Italy has been concerned about widespread illegality in investments throughout Italy, with specific reference to money coming from drug trafficking and in particular from 'ndrangheta clans (Visco 2014). Warning about the difficult quantifications of the mafia phenomenon and even more of the illegal economy linked to the mafia phenomenon, Banca d'Italia estimated in 2012 that the illegal economy represents in Italy 10 % of total GDP (Ardizzi et al. 2012). These numbers call for a careful observation of the movements of the amount of money that Calabrian clans can dispose of through their illegal activities—especially once we have observed their primary role in the international drug trade.

According to the DNA (2015: 402), any mafia economy is characterised by a *"very high return of investment"*: for cocaine trafficking only, for example, *"to an investment of 100,000 Euros in purchases correspond a return of at least 300,000 in sale after distribution"*. Not only cocaine represents a very lucrative business but it also explains why the 'ndrangheta clans—for whom cocaine is the first source of revenues—are willing to acquire a monopoly in the trade and to establish connections and alliances with those in the territories of production. The "mafia entrepreneur" can accept the risks associated to its activity in consideration of the higher profits (Gottschalk 2009; Siegel and van de Bunt 2012a, b).

In Antimafia operations, money laundering represents a necessary evergreen of mafia activities. Indeed, it is crucial for the clans to be able to (re)invest and camouflage the money from the drug trade, usually in legal businesses and/or in other services. According to the analysts of the Central Service for Organised Crime Investigations within the Italian fiscal police, the 'ndrangheta clans need to resort to very complex money laundering schemes to clean all the money from cocaine trafficking (Magliocco 2012). The clans use both banks and financial intermediaries to proceed with their investments in order to clean the drug money. As consistently indicated by the most recent reports of the National Antimafia Directorate (DNA 2014; DNA 2011; DNA 2015; DNA 2012) and the fiscal police (Magliocco 2012), 'ndrangheta clans tend to adapt to business trends through specialisation, growth, expansion within national and international markets, and relationships with other clans. Over the years, the 'ndrangheta clans have invested in a variety of sectors, such as hotels, restaurants, import–export companies, food companies, tourist activities and services, and real estate (Calderoni 2011; Calderoni et al. 2015). This is encapsulated in the words of a mafia boss, Antonino Pesce, video-recorded during Operation All Clean.[18] He is talking about his son Francesco:

> He [indicating his son] he knows how to do this, he is inside, he knows what goes and what doesn't, from the garage to the shops, no one can fool him, he makes money, he puts third persons in [in the management of the shops], cannot put relatives, that would ruin him, but others can manage well. You have to buy and sell, [do you] understand? [...] He has become a businessman, an investor, but not here, everywhere, not in Rosarno, there's nothing else in Rosarno, maybe racket, drugs, this stuff, but he managed to get inside there [he indicates the North with his hand], this is what he has become.

If investments in the legal economy are the necessary steps for well established '*ndrine*, investments abroad guarantee even more the possibility to elude controls and confiscations. During Operation New Bridge,[19] an undercover FBI agent reported about a meeting in Brooklyn, where members of the clan Ursino were discussing a proposal for a money laundering operation of 11 million euros from cocaine trafficking. This was not the first and only scheme of this type abroad. Operation Buongustaio revealed important information about a money laundering scheme with the support of members of a criminal organisation based in the UK.[20] Operation Metropolis[21] had also seen the interests of the clan Morabito from Africo and the clan Aquino from Gioiosa Ionica, both on the East coast of the province of Reggio Calabria, to invest in Ireland and in the UK through "smurf" deposits in bank accounts, loan back operations, establishment of trusts, investments in property development through colluded solicitors in London, and securitisation of credits for third-party investments. The role of partners in European countries is key to keep the money close enough to Calabria but still far enough to be disguised.

Data on money laundering and investments of the clans, especially abroad, are difficult to collect. They usually are tied to the properties confiscated within Antimafia proceedings or they can be obtained by following suspicious activity reports related to the drug trade. During Operation Gambling,[22] law enforcement matched investments abroad with the proceeds of drug trades in Calabria, or through Calabria in the Antilles, in the Canary Islands, in Malta, in Romania, in Slovenia, in Egypt, and in Australia. Most of these laundering schemes had been operated through fictitious foreign ownership of assets facilitated by lawyers, accountants, and financial mediators both in Italy and abroad. In the confirmation of the charges for Operation Gambling, the Tribunal in Reggio Calabria[23] observes how the events object of investigations include:

> All the 'ndrangheta clans, with an operational strategy close to a corporation, all new, aiming at a progressive normalisation and legalisation of their own activities, at the maximisation of profits. On the one side they set the economic grounds and organise the practical conditions to systematically launder the proceeds of crimes; on the other side, they manage to use these bases and conditions into new occasions to make more money.

CONCLUSION

The Calabrian clans, as demonstrated by numerous Antimafia Operations, can count on qualified brokers who have privileged relationships with the various producers and distributors of cocaine in North, Central, and South America. Also, the presence of 'ndrangheta members has been observed in all the major port cities around Europe and Latin America. In the past years, the clans have been dominant players in the drug market, especially the cocaine market. Through their brokers, they have played the peculiar role of mediators with sellers in countries of production in Latin America. They also oversee various stages of the importations to Europe: from the loading of drugs in the various American ports, to their arrival, clearance, and distribution to different criminal groups in various European ports.

As seen in the latest investigations, the presence of '*ndrine* or individuals linked to 'ndrangheta clans has been ascertained in countries where consumption of drugs is high (like Canada, the USA, and Australia) and in countries where drugs usually transit the most (the Netherlands, Germany, and Spain) (UNODC 2015). The authorities have repeatedly warned about the ability of the clans to handle cocaine trafficking because of their reticular presence in the Western countries. Their international presence, as discussed in this chapter, is also supported by the need and will to reinvest the money from the drug trade through various laundering schemes that allow avoiding national legislations and confiscations.

In this chapter, finally, we argued that the international presence of the clans linked to drug trade and money laundering cannot be understood without engaging in a deeper analysis of the local dimension of drug trafficking. The port of Gioia Tauro and more generally the entrenched dominion over people and spaces in Calabria is what has allowed the clans to prosper and become "reliable" drug traffickers, through a minimisation of risks and a maximisation of profits. In drug trafficking, the nature of the 'ndrangheta as *plural* phenomenon is quite clearly visible: on the one hand, the clans can make their own fortune abroad through the '*ndranghetisation* process of clans having various origins in Calabria who can use a respected brand name. On the other hand, the existence of coordination structures and shared set of behaviours, especially at the local level, allows to minimise risks and overcome problems and conflicts.

NOTES

1. Albeit established by Constitution in 1947, the first regional elections with the effective establishment of regions in Italy only happened in 1970.
2. Operation Olimpia, No. 104/95 R.G.N.R. DDA + No. 85/96 R.G. G.I.P. DDA, Court of Assizes No. 15/98 R.G., sentence No.3/2001 R.G.
3. Operation Decollo I, No. 1779-6541/2001 + 3164/2002 + 1429/2003 R.G.N.R. DDA + No. 2523-8748/2001 + 2085-2086/2003 R.G. GIP.
4. Operation Decollo I, No. 1779-6541/2001 + 3164/2002 + 1429/2003 R.G.N.R. DDA + No. 2523-8748/2001 + 2085-2086/2003 R.G. GIP, p. 33.
5. Operation Decollo I, No. 1779-6541/2001 + 3164/2002 + 1429/2003 R.G.N.R. DDA + No. 2523-8748/2001 + 2085-2086/2003 R.G. GIP, p. 402.

6. Interview in Reggio Calabria, DDA Procura della Repubblica, 16 December 2015, translated from Italian.
7. "Seven Sisters" was a term coined in the 1950s by Enrico Mattei, then head of the Italian state oil company Eni, to describe the seven oil companies that formed the "Consortium for Iran" cartel and dominated the global petroleum industry from the mid-1940s to the 1970s.
8. Operation New Bridge, No. 3273/12 R.G.N.R. DDA.
9. Operation Buongustaio, No. 8354/2010 R.G.N.R. DDA + No. 5084/2011 R.G. GIP.
10. US District Court E.D.N.Y. F. #2014R00552.
11. Operation Columbus II, No. 2082/2014 R.G.N.R. DDA.
12. Operation Solares II, No. 611/2008 R.G.N.R. DDA.
13. Operation All Inside, No. 4302/06 R.G.N.R. DDA.
14. Operation All Inside, No. 4302/06 R.G.N.R. DDA, p. 528.
15. Operation Buongustaio, No. 8354/2010 R.G.N.R. DDA + No. 5084/2011 R.G. GIP + No. 11/2014 R.G.N.R. DDA.
16. Operation All Inside, No. 4302/06 R.G.N.R. DDA.
17. Operation All Inside, No. 4302/06 R.G.N.R. DDA.
18. Operation All Clean, No. 9762/11 R.G.N.R. DDA + No. 4302/06 R.G.N.R. DDA, p. 612.
19. Operation New Bridge, No. 3273/12 R.G.N.R. DDA, p. 57.
20. Operation Buongustaio, No. 8354/2010 R.G.N.R. DDA, p. 272.
21. Operation Metropolis, No. 3369/2008 R.G.N.R. DDA.
22. Operation Gambling, No. 7497/14 R.G.R.N. DDA.
23. Operation Gambling, No. 7497/14 R.G.R.N. DDA, p. 46.

References

Ardizzi, G., Petraglia, C., Piacenza, M., et al. (2012). Measuring the underground economy with the currency demand approach: A reinterpretation of the methodology, with an application to Italy. *Banca d'Italia Temi di Discussione* 864.

Banca d'Italia. (2015). Economie regionali. L'economia della Calabria. In: Eurosistema BdI (ed). Catanzaro.

Calderoni, F. (2011). Where is the mafia in Italy? Measuring the presence of the mafia across Italian provinces. *Global Crime, 12*(1), 41–69.

Calderoni, F. (2012). The structure of drug trafficking mafias: The 'Ndrangheta and cocaine. *Crime, Law and Social Change, 58*(3), 321–349.

Calderoni, F., Berlusconi, G., Garofalo, L., et al. (2015). The Italian mafias in the world: A systematic assessment of the mobility of criminal groups. *European Journal of Criminology.* doi:10.1177/1477370815623570.

Campos, A. C. (2014, March 20). Brazil's Federal Police launches anti-drugs operation in nine countries. *Agencia Brasil EBC* (http://agenciabrasil.ebc.com.br/en/geral/noticia/2014-03/brazils-federal-police-launches-anti-drugs-operation-nine-countries).

Cingari, G. (1982). *Storia della Calabria dall'Unità a Oggi*. Bari: Editori Laterza.

DNA. (2011). *Relazione annuale sulle attività svolte dal Procuratore Nazionale Antimafia e dalla Direzione Nazionale Antimafia nonché sulle dinamiche e strategie della criminalità organizzata di tipo mafioso*. Rome: Direzione Nazionale Antimafia.

DNA. (2012). *Relazione annuale sulle attività svolte dal Procuratore Nazionale Antimafia e dalla Direzione Nazionale Antimafia nonché sulle dinamiche e strategie della criminalità organizzata di tipo mafioso*. Rome: Direzione Nazionale Antimafia.

DNA. (2014). *Relazione annuale sulle attività svolte dal Procuratore Nazionale Antimafia e dalla Direzione Nazionale Antimafia nonché sulle dinamiche e strategie della criminalità organizzata di tipo mafioso*. Rome: Direzione Nazionale Antimafia.

DNA. (2015). *Relazione annuale sulle attività svolte dal Procuratore Nazionale Antimafia e dalla Direzione Nazionale Antimafia nonché sulle dinamiche e strategie della criminalità organizzata di tipo mafioso*. Rome: Direzione Nazionale Antimafia.

DNA. (2016). *Relazione annuale sulle attività svolte dal Procuratore nazionale e dalla Direzione nazionale antimafia e antiterrorismo nonché sulle dinamiche e strategie della criminalità organizzata di tipo mafioso*. Roma: Direzione Nazionale Antimafia e Antiterrorismo.

FBI. (2014). Twenty-Four Defendants with Ties to Powerful Italian Organized Crime Syndicate Known as the 'Ndrangheta Arrested in Coordinated U.S.-Italian Takedown In: FBI New York Field Office (ed). https://http://www.fbi.gov/newyork/press-releases/2014/twenty-four-defendants-with-ties-to-powerful-italian-organized-crime-syndicate-known-as-the-ndrangheta-arrested-in-coordinated-u.s.-italian-takedown.

Forgione, F. (2008). Relazione Annuale sulla 'Ndrangheta. In: *Commissione Parlamentare d'inchiesta sul fenomeno della mafia e sulle altre associazioni criminali as* (ed). Roma.

Gambino, S. (1975). *La Mafia in Calabria*. Reggio Calabria: Edizioni Parallelo.

Gottschalk, P. (2009). *Entrepreneurship and organised crime: Entrepreneurs in illegal business*. Cheltenham: Edward Elgar.

Gratteri, N., & Nicaso, A. (2015). *Oro bianco*. Milan: Mondadori.

Magliocco, G. (2012). Guardia di Finanza: Metodologie e Strumenti di Contrasto alla Criminalità Organizzata. *Audizione Presso La Commissione Speciale del Parlamento Europeo sulla Criminalità Organizzata, la Corruzione e il Riciclaggio di Denaro (CRIM)*. Rome 31 October 2012.

Senato della Repubblica. (2015). *Relazione sull'Attività svolta e sui Risultati conseguiti dalla Direzione Investigativa Antimafia* (Primo Semestre 2014). 13 January 2015.

Sergi, A. (2015, August). Faimily Fortunes: Calabrian mafia extends its international reach. *Jane's Intelligence Review*: 41–44.

Sergi, A. (2016). "Three Tales/Two Threats". Prosecutors in Italy, England and the United States narrate national and transnational organised crime. In: P.C. Van Duyne, A. Maljević, G. A. Antonopoulos, et al. (eds) *Cross Border Crime Colloquium 2015*. Oisterwijk: Wolf Legal Publishers.

Sergi, P. (1988). Sulla Via dell'Eroina. Dalla Calabria agli USA. *La Repubblica*. 3 April 1988.

Sergi, P. (1991). *La "Santa" Violenta*. Cosenza: Periferia.

Siegel, D., & van de Bunt, H. (2012). *Traditional organized crime in the modern world: Responses to socioeconomic change*. New York: Springer.

SOS Impresa. (2012). *XIII Rapporto. Le mani della criminalità sulle imprese*. Rome.

UIF. (2015). Rapporto Annuale dell'Unità di Informazione Finanziaria. *Unità di Informazione Finanziaria per l'Italia*. Roma: Banca D'Italia.

UNODC. (2015). *World Drug Report*. New York: United Nations.

Visco, I. (2014). Contrasto all'economia criminale: precondizione per la crescita economica. In: Guardia di Finanza (ed) *Convegno Banca d'Italia—Fondazione Cirgis*. Rome. 7 November 2014: Available for download http://www.bancaditalia.it/pubblicazioni/interventi-governatore/integov2014/visco-071114.pdf.

CHAPTER 6

Poly-crime 'Ndrangheta

Abstract The 'ndrangheta is a poly-crime mafia. This second chapter of Part II looks at various illicit markets the clans invest in and are protagonist of, presenting some selected and relevant cases to show the versatility and the flexibility of illegal activities of the Calabrian clans today. The first part of the chapter focuses on case studies of criminal activities of the 'ndrangheta linked to the environment, in Calabria but not only, namely illegal waste disposal, waste trafficking, and investments in renewable energies. The other sections of the chapter will look at the latest investigations in sectors such as the fruit, vegetable and flower markets, gambling, and migrant smuggling.

Keywords Poly-Crime 'Ndrangheta • Green Economy • Environmental Crimes and Migrants Smuggling • Online Gambling

INTRODUCTION

'Ndrangheta clans are a very good example of poly-crime criminal groups, versatile and entrepreneurial enough to quickly and successfully move among different criminal markets by seizing emerging opportunities. Their flexibility allows them to succeed in a broad range of profit-making criminal ventures, as well as in money laundering activities to fund new activities. In Calabria, the clans engage in usury, fraud schemes, extortion, procurement of public contracts, and embezzlement

© The Editor(s) (if applicable) and The Author(s) 2016
A. Sergi, A. Lavorgna, *'Ndrangheta,*
DOI 10.1007/978-3-319-32585-9_6

and exploitation of European funds just to name a few activities (DNA 2015). Their presence has a severe impact on the regional economy and delays development and innovation actions in the territory, while confirming the deep social bond of the 'ndrangheta with the Calabrian territory (Sergi and South 2016). Also outside their homeland, both in Italy and abroad, the ability of the clans to penetrate the socio-economic textures of their new settlements has led to great profit-making opportunities.

The first two sections of this chapter will focus on case studies of criminal activities linked to the environment and to the green economy in Italy, namely illegal waste disposal, waste trafficking, and investments in renewable energies. The reason to focus on these aspects lies in the alarm raised by Italian authorities and NGOs warning how Calabria and other Italian regions where the 'ndrangheta has successfully settled—such as Lombardia—are in a very dangerous position when it comes to environmental hazards. Furthermore, these crimes severely interfere with the economic development of the country more generally, often resulting in corruption, bad management of public funds, and inadequate or even dangerous constructions and infrastructures (Sergi and South 2016). The final sections of the chapter will focus instead on demonstrating the extreme versatility of the clans by looking at recent investigations in sectors as diverse as the markets of fruit, vegetable and flowers, gambling, and migrant smuggling.

DIRTY BUSINESS: TURNING WASTE INTO PROFIT

Environmental crimes have become increasingly important for policy makers, the general public, and researchers around the world. The harm they pose is multifaceted, and affects all parts of society. In Italy, mafia groups have traditionally been very active in this domain, to the point that the term "ecomafia" has been coined by the Italian NGO Legambiente (Legambiente 2016). Investigations over poor waste management and the presence of illegal dumping sites hit the news daily. To maximise profits, illegal waste dumping occurs sometimes in connection with soil mining to meet the demand of the construction and infrastructure section; this is how mining sites become dumping sites, as illegally filled with waste (Commissione Parlamentare di Inchiesta 2000a; Legambiente 2014; Rege and Lavorgna 2016).

With the exception of waste trafficking (art.260 of the legislative decree 152/2006) and waste burning (art.265-*bis* of the legislative decree 152/2006 as introduced by the law 6/2014), environmental crimes were generally considered not as serious crimes but only as misdemeanours within the Italian legal framework. As a consequence, sanctions were fairly low, and prescription limits expired quickly (Commissione Parlamentare d'Inchiesta 2012), making these criminal activities high reward and low risk for criminal groups. Only recently, in May 2015, the Parliament approved a new law on the introduction of environmental crimes into the Criminal Code, categorising them as felonies (Lavorgna 2015a).

Several law enforcement investigations—such as Operations Black Mountains,[1] Rifiuti S.p.A I[2] and II[3]—demonstrated how the 'ndrangheta plays a major role in environmental crimes in its homeland. As explained in Chap. 2, the control of the 'ndrangheta clans over their homeland Calabria remains incredibly tight. As reported in the last Legambiente report (2015), 9.3 % of all environmental crimes in Italy occur in Calabria, and more specifically 7.7 % of waste-related crimes and 12.2 % of crimes related to the construction and earthmover sectors. Concerning the waste sector, historically the clans operated a *de facto* control, based on intimidation, social consensus, and collusion with the public administration (Commissione Parlamentare di Inchiesta 2000b; Ruggiero and South 2010). Lately, in line with the '*ndranghetisation* process—which sees the clans more aggressively using the power of their brand to reinforce their presence over illegal markets in Calabria, Italy, and abroad—there is increased evidence of their direct acquisition of firms operating in the sector: besides intimidation and protection rackets, the clans' entrepreneurial power rest on their economic capacity in a territory afflicted by poverty and unemployment (DNA 2016).

As recently reminded by Sergi and South (2016), the clans' involvement in the waste business is an issue not only of control of the territory but also of slackness in control and policing from local authorities. Indeed, in Calabria there are structural problems—for example, the geographical seclusion of certain municipalities—that make waste collection problematic. Serious efforts and expensive investment would be required. However, current interventions have solely attempted to enlarge older and overfilled dumps or open new ones without really addressing the problem at its roots, for instance by investing in recycling. In Calabria, there has not been a systematic policy in place for over 20 years. In the early 1990s, almost 50 million euros were allocated to the creation of new waste management system, but the target was not met (Commissione Parlamentare di Inchiesta 2000b; Commissione Parlamentare di Inchiesta 2000a).

The emergency status was declared for Calabria in 1997, with special powers granted to the Governor. The emergency status was supposed to last for a limited amount of time to give the region the tools to stand on its own feet with regard to waste management. It has been almost two decades, but the "emergency" has not been solved yet: criticism has been raised towards the effectiveness of the compulsory administration—accused of lack of transparency and honesty—and the "not in my backyard attitude" by the people of Calabria, who opposed development plans if too close to their properties (Commissione Parlamentare di Inchiesta 2011; Pracchi et al. 2012). The latest publication of the Antimafia Directorate reports that in the Reggio Calabria hinterland alone the waste business is worth a total of 150 million euros per year (equals to the 2 % of the GDP of the territory); considering the pervasiveness of the 'ndrangheta in the area, it is baffling that (at least until a few years ago) only 12 out of 161 business companies involved in the sector had obtained administrative anti-mafia certificates (DNA 2015). The certificates, which private companies need in Italy to carry out work or provide services or goods to public entities, attest that an individual or company is not subject to any security measures applied together with a charge or indictments for unlawful association offences (DNA 2013).

The way in which the clans can take advantage of this situation is twofold. First, current policies largely depend on the practical ability to realise and manage new dumping sites. The clans have traditionally been heavily involved in the construction and earthmover sectors, and along the years, they have been found responsible for unauthorised excavations, illegal activities against the landscape, and frauds against public administration for the construction of public works (Commissione Parlamentare di Inchiesta 2011; Lavorgna 2015a; Sergi and South 2016). In areas where the mafia presence is rooted, legitimate firms often simply avoid competing or confronting mafia-infiltrated firms as they would experience retaliation (Commissione Parlamentare d'Inchiesta 2012; Rege and Lavorgna 2016).

Second, clans have been at the centre of regional, national, and transnational investigations connected to the waste cycle, including trafficking of toxic waste and illegal dumping sites: safely processing and storing waste from industries can cost even thousands of euros per ton, making illegal disposal highly profitable. For instance, in the late 1990s, clans from the Cosenza area, in the north of the region, were dumping hazardous waste coming from the Crotone area (in the north-east) in agricultural areas, disguised with household waste (Commissione Parlamentare di Inchiesta 2000a). At that time, the clans were deemed to be very active in this criminal activity for the limited risks it entailed, being sanctions only administrative and not criminal. However, notwithstanding the new regulations, illegal dumping and trafficking of toxic waste continue (Legambiente 2015). Operations Black Mountain[4] perfectly exemplifies the way in which the clans can doubly take advantage of the construction/waste connection, with the illegal disposal of toxic waste—namely *cubilot* slag containing highly carcinogenic metals—in the material used to build public infrastructures near Crotone thanks to the connivance of the local administration (Pracchi et al. 2012). As noticed by the Parliamentary Commission for Inquiry into illegal activities linked to waste management, Operation Black Mountain is *"an exemplary case, and an objective one, where a 'twisted economy', by breaching the law, not only has provoked an environmental damage, but has prevailed over elementary rules on competition and fair politics, destroying the 'healthy economy'"* (Commissione Parlamentare di Inchiesta 2011: 141).

Beside the mainland, also the sea around Calabria represents a cause of concern, with the port of Gioia Tauro playing a key role also in the transnational trafficking of waste, especially towards Africa, India, and China (Commissione Parlamentare di Inchiesta 2000a; Commissione Parlamentare di Inchiesta 2011; Pergolizzi 2012). Particularly worrisome is the case of the so-called *navi dei veleni* ("poison ships") o *navi a perdere* ("ships to be lost"); allegedly, 39 vessels suspiciously sunk in deep waters around Calabrian coasts in the 1980s and early 1990s while transporting toxic and radioactive material. Their locations are still investigated, but the endeavour is expensive and has been slow, despite the significant consequences for the health of the population, the local ecosystem, and the fishing industry. To maximise profits, in certain cases the accidental sinking of old but registered vessels was faked in order to get additional money from frauding insurance companies (Commissione Parlamentare di Inchiesta 2000b; Commissione Parlamentare di Inchiesta 2000a; Chiavari 2011; Sergi and South 2016).

'Ndrangheta clans have been active in environmental crimes also outside their homeland. The case of Lombardia is of particular interest, even if it should be noted that other northern regions, such as Piemonte, exhibit similar phenomena (CROSS 2015). In Lombardia, the situation has long been underestimated. For instance, the Commissione Parlamentare d'Inchiesta (Commissione Parlamentare di Inchiesta 1999: 360) reported that *"the situation [...] is overall normal and conform to the existing legislation [...] What is worrisome is the role of Lombardia as 'sender' of the waste, then disposed in other regions."* However, a number of law enforcement operations over the last decade demystified this outdated, optimistic view, and demonstrated the extent and the pervasiveness of the 'ndrangheta clans in the region also with regard to crimes affecting the environment. As reported by the Commissione Parlamentare d'Inchiesta (2012), since 2001, with the passing of a new anti-mafia law against waste-related crimes, about 10 % of all inquiries were recorded in the Milano hinterland, with severe cases of illegal dumping especially in the Milano and Brescia areas.

The strong relationship between waste crimes (and especially the illegal dumping of toxic waste) and the earthmover and construction sectors is particularly evident in this area as well, as demonstrated by recent law enforcement operations such as Cerberus,[5] Isola,[6] Parco Sud I and II,[7] Tenacia,[8] and Redux-Caposaldo.[9] The Commissione Parlamentare d'Inchiesta (2012) estimated that up to 70 % of the firms operating in the earthmover and constructions sector in Lombardia appears to be linked to 'ndrangheta clans.

Clans can operate direct management over the earthmoving sector by means of public contracts and subcontracts so that workers remain under the control of the clans (Commissione Parlamentare d'Inchiesta 2012; Rege and Lavorgna 2016). In this way, moreover, the clans can use the earthmover sector as a source of political influence: clans can rely on these workers—generally from Calabria—as potential voters and therefore as political leverage tool (Commissione Parlamentare d'Inchiesta 2012). Legal firms winning construction tenders might be forced to rely on smaller ones, controlled by the clans, for necessary stages of the activity, where significant manpower but little expertise is necessary (Sciarrone 2001; Chiavari 2011; Rege and Lavorgna 2016). Also, real ownership of resources is often disguised through figureheads (Commissione Parlamentare d'Inchiesta 2012). Workers non-affiliated with the clans do not press charges out of fear of retaliation. Also, in the North, the mafia method of violence and intimidation is majorly effective thanks to the reputation of the Calabrian clans. For instance, between 2009 and 2012 in Lombardia alone, more than 70 intimidating acts featuring weapons and explosives were recorded, but most victims did not file complaints (Commissione Parlamentare d'Inchiesta 2012).

Corruption is used to obtain access to public tenders systematically or occasionally, to deal with public administration, and allegedly to make sure that law enforcement officers do not control over certain trucks (Commissione Parlamentare d'Inchiesta 2012; Rege and Lavorgna 2016). Furthermore, clans are very successful in exploiting legal loopholes; as stressed by the Antimafia Directorate, their modus operandi has been perfected over time (DNA 2015; DNA 2014; DNA 2012). As emerged, for instance, from operations Redux-Caposaldo[10] and Isola,[11] clans can obtain haulage licences on behalf of a third party to circumvent the administrative anti-mafia certificate. In addition, documents such as the logbooks of truck drivers are regularly falsified with regard to the type and the amount of material transported by trucks (Rege and Lavorgna 2016). While these tactics are not particularly sophisticated, they need to rely on complex systems comprising different people with technical, operative, and administrative roles in order to function properly.

Firms run or supported by the clans are able to lower the prices because of their disrespect of regulations, which is attractive for operators in the legal economy trying to minimise costs and maximise profits, especially in the light of the economic and financial crisis that hit also Italy over the last decade that has harshly affected also the construction sector (Lavorgna 2015a). Alongside people affiliated to the clans, investigations showed the involvement of people well integrated in the legal economy in the legal waste disposal and in the earthmover sectors, that in certain cases appeared actively supporting the modus operandi of the clans to increase their share of profits (Commissione Parlamentare d'Inchiesta 2012; Rege and Lavorgna 2016).

GOING GREEN: INVESTING IN RENEWABLE ENERGIES

As anticipated in Chap. 2, Calabria is underdeveloped in terms of economic growth and it highly depends on public expenditure. In recent years, thanks to the EU support, the region has been investing in the green economy and specifically in renewable energies, with 68 open projects on wind power and 416 on photovoltaic in 2015 (Sergi and South 2016). After all, renewable energy has been on the world's political agenda since the mid-1990s, and the EU has supported several actions to support the development of green economy (Caneppele et al. 2013). As recently reminded by Sergi and South (2016), Calabria is one of the convergence areas benefitting from EU structural cohesion, development and social funds and policies; within the EU Regional Policy, being the region's GDP pro capita below 75 % of the EU average, Calabria is among the top objectives of intervention. As it emerges from the data aggregated by Open Coesione, an online portal on the use and allocation of structural funds in Italy, a total of 517.3 million euros have been invested in Calabria, with 1371 open projects (Open Coesione 2016) in the last cycle of EU intervention as of February 2016. Environment-related protection and innovation activity in Calabria is the second highest-ranking category of intervention and allocation of structural funds, following transport (Open Coesione 2016; Sergi and South 2016).

The green economy, however, is today not only a very lucrative and growing business for the domestic and foreign companies that compete for investments, but it can be very profitable also for the clans. As explained by Sergi and South (2016), the economic benefits of an installation that produces electric energy from renewable sources are linked to the allocation of both public funds and incentives and the sale or self-consumption of the energy. In Calabria, however, the very complex bureaucracy required to have the projects assigned and the lack of control in monitoring the projects once funds have been allocated is deemed to create legal loopholes and opportunities for criminal infiltration and money laundering (Caneppele et al. 2013). In addition, because of the administrative burdens, many approved projects are obsolete even before they are realised, which leaves room for malpractices (Pracchi et al. 2012).

The wind power business, for instance, can be very lucrative through the construction of wind farms, and Calabria has a great wind potential (Caneppele et al. 2013). In Isola di Capo Rizzuto, near Crotone, there was one of the biggest wind park in Europe, with 48 wind blades and a total value estimated in a few hundred million euros. The park was seized in 2012 by a law enforcement operation targeting, among others, the Arena clan, suspected of using the park for money laundering (DNA 2012). Between January 2014 and December 2015, Operations Kyterion I and II shed light on the interests of the Grande Aracri clan towards a major wind park near Crotone, managed through a system of subcontracts enforced through extortion and intimidation (DNA 2016). As noticed by one of the prosecutors in charge of the investigations, still ongoing:

> This clan is peculiar, they are as powerful as some of the Reggio clans, they are respected, and they are well known. They have their facilitators who work on their investments, like this wind park. It's about trusting who works

for you, it's a system based on reputation and enforcement of agreements, so that things work and no-one has problems.[12]

The interferences with the EU structural funds are the result of both a rational planning of clans to invest in a very lucrative business and the greed of the elite of public administrators that allow criminal infiltration through corruption (Sergi and South 2016). The line between mafia and the ruling elite can be particularly thin in this domain, with the risk of twisting the promising aspects of the green economy into a wasted opportunity. Operation Naos from the Special Unit ROS of the Carabinieri in Perugia, Umbria region (DIA 2008), for instance, exposed the involvement of the Morabito–Palamara–Bruzzaniti clan in public procurement in other Italian regions such as Umbria and their investments in touristic areas and in hydroelectric plants in the Reggio Calabria hinterland. From the investigation, the role of local politicians emerged as a key factor in allowing the clans getting access to public funds (CNEL 2012). We read in an intercepted conversation widely distributed by the media at the time that a Calabrian boss was talking to the elected counsellor (afterwards arrested) for Tourism in the Regional Committee in Calabria about other politicians in Umbria who approached the criminal clans (Toscano 2008):

> If we were gullible they wouldn't let us do it; they know they can earn money through us, you know? I wouldn't have thought by myself to call them and say 'hey counsellor, sign this for me and not for others' [...] And now, they are in our hands, you know?

Because of political involvement, public funds can be diverted from their original scope through corruption or even fraud; even when the projects are completed, they are often deficient, hence failing to boost innovation and promote convergence (Sergi and South 2016). It is not surprising that a key role in allowing the 'ndrangheta infiltration in the green economy is played by the so-called grey area formed by companies and professionals that might be not directly part of the clans but that nonetheless enjoy a mutually beneficial relationship with them. For instance, the CNEL (2012) and the DNA (2012) underlined how investigations suggested that project developers might be particularly at risk of criminal infiltration because of their privileged relationship with local elites, and their capacity to dialogue with the technical, administrative, and entrepreneurial partners of the funded project.

NOT ONLY DRUGS: A GLANCE INTO THE FOOD
AND FLOWERS MARKETS

'Ndrangheta clans, as in the case of other Italian mafias, demonstrated a remarkable ability in infiltrating the strategic agricultural sector, as well as the wholesale distribution sector. After all, Italian mafias historically have been closely linked to agriculture (Arlacchi 1986; Lupo 2009) and the term "agromafia" has been coined to emphasise their connections with the farming and food industry (Eurispes 2015). Not only does agriculture allow the clans to strengthen their territorial control throughout the whole food chain, from production to distribution, but also it permits unjust enrichment through frauds. For instance, citrus production is a key agricultural sector in Calabria, with about one fourth of the total national production concentrated in this region (SOS Impresa 2012). The infamous "paper oranges" scandal in 2010 shed light on the systemic fraud towards EU funds carried out under the guise of the Bellocco clan in Rosarno (near Reggio Calabria), with the declared production of oranges being up to ten times more than in reality; as a consequence, the EU changed its funding criteria—from harvest quantity to surface of production (EU Committee on Civil Liberties 2010).

Concerning distribution markets, in Calabria, Operations Araba Fenice,[13] Reggio Sud,[14] and Sistema-Assenzio[15] among others proved how clans infiltrated the food distribution system in the area of Reggio Calabria (Commissione di Accesso 2012; DNA 2015; DNA 2014; DNA 2012). Besides being a valuable market and convenient for money laundering purposes, the food distribution sector requires the clans to engage with the local entrepreneurial and political actors for mutual benefit. These contacts facilitate the practice of *"assunzioni clientelari"*—that is, influence peddling and cronyism in hiring—which has also consequence in terms of political influence in the territory and *"allows to widen the reach of the mafia contamination more and more, to the point of distorting the job market"*.[16]

Considering this convergence of interests around the wholesale distribution sector, it is not surprising how this model was replicated in areas of colonisation, such as Lombardia. Here, as it emerged for instance during Operation For a King (CROSS 2015), the food market was used also to camouflage other illicit traffics, first and foremost cocaine trafficking: the Morabito clan from the Reggio Calabria hinterland was involved in a major route for trafficking cocaine from South America to Europe, from

Buenos Aires to Milano via Dakar. Through a system of cooperatives and subcontracts, the clan was operating in the fruit market of Milano, one of the major ones in Europe, while maintaining relationships with local politicians.

Furthermore, some recent cases involving Calabrian clans in the Netherlands contribute to explain the great flexibility and adaptability of the '*ndrine* and the role of import–export societies in facilitating money laundering and in furthering possibilities for investments from the clans. Operations Acero[17] in Reggio Calabria, Krupy[18] in Rome in September 2015, and Levinius in the Netherlands (carried out by the National Crime Squad) in October 2014 have demonstrated the ability of clans from Siderno, in the East Coast of the Reggio Calabria province (also known for their links to clans in Canada and Australia, as seen in Chap. 4) in diversifying their activities abroad through the flower industry. Members of the Crupi clan from Siderno were operative in Latina, near Roma, through the firm KRUPI s.r.l. They were also controlling Fresh B.V., a firm operating in the flower business in Aalsmeer, North Holland. The clan was collecting cash money in Calabria, Sicilia, and Campania, sending it to Latina, and from there to the Netherlands hidden in flower trucks; in the Netherlands, they collected cocaine to be distributed in the Italian market (in Milano and Roma) hidden in the same trucks together with flowers, which were therefore used both for camouflage and for money laundering. The court orders[19] describe the clan as highly organised and stable and their operations as systematic and very frequent: it is likely that law enforcement operations discovered just the tip of the iceberg and that the flower business is extensively used to cover drug trafficking activities in the Netherlands (DNA 2016). In the same investigations, the authorities have also uncovered a "sweet" business related to possession and selling of stolen Lindt chocolate, also orchestrated in between the Netherlands, Canada, Siderno in Calabria, and in the hinterland of Milano and Roma. The chocolate (approximately 250 tons, for a value of 7.5 million euros) had been stolen in 2014 from the premises of the company Lindt Italia in Lodi, near Milano, fenced by affiliated to the clan, and then sold to third parties.[20]

GAMBLING, FRAUDS, AND THE LEISURE INDUSTRY

In Italy, despite the economic and financial crisis that severely hit the country, the gambling industry is on the rise, with a prevalence of slot machines and video lotteries, followed by traditional lotteries, sport bets, bingos, and skill games, for a turnover up to 80 billion euros per year (DNA 2012). Legal gambling is strictly regulated by the State. Through a system of licences, dealers have to meet certain requirements and are then authorised to manage the gambling business through a physical infrastructure or online.

In the former case, the gamer needs to be identified if he wins more than 1000 euros. Clans can clone video poker machines or tamper with slot machines that transmit information to the relevant national authority for tax purposes, for instance by manipulating their software, hence committing a serious fraud against the State (Sergi and Lavorgna 2012). 'Ndrangheta clans and corrupted entrepreneurs have imposed their machines to dealers in Calabria, but also in Veneto, Piemonte, Lombardia, Emilia Romagna, and Germany (SOS Impresa 2011; Annibaldi and Tocco 2010; DNA 2012), as it emerges, for instance, by the above-mentioned Operation Redux-Caposaldo[21] and Famiglia Valle.[22]

Regarding online games, according to Italian law, every better has to identify him/herself by providing his/her personal details and ID number in order to receive an individual username and password. The bet will partially return to the gamers if he/she wins, partially go to the State as tax revenue, and partially remain to the dealer (DNA 2012). Foreign gambling operators are allowed to operate online real money games, but before offering their services to Italian citizens, they need to get an Italian licence. If the bet occurs in a website that is not under this system (for instance, if the website has .com rather than .it as domain extension, suggesting that the servers are controlled from outside the Italian jurisdiction), it is possible for criminal networks to speculate on the tax revenues; also, this way they can avoid the stringent regulations imposed by Italian laws, disrespecting the legal safeguards for the gamers.

The involvement of 'ndrangheta clans in the leisure industry, and particularly in the online betting sector, is an important indicator of their evolution and sophistication, and of their capacity—even if not fully expressed yet (Lavorgna and Sergi 2014; Lavorgna 2015b)—to exploit online crime opportunities. For instance, Operation Black Monkey[23] (from the name of a counterfeit card used for slot machines) clearly described the entrepreneurial features of the clans from the Reggio Calabria hinterland—able to launder money from the one side, while increasing their profits on the other—also in partnership with clans from the Neapolitan Camorra. Besides commercialising tampered slot machines, the clans were involved in a system of illegal online gambling that was exploiting gaps between the

Italian, the Romanian, and the UK legislation to boost profits. It is particularly interesting, in this operation, to notice the clans' capacity not only to infiltrate the trade but also to mingle with entrepreneurs in it, to act from the inside, taking control without being noticed. Intimidation can be subtle, and the 'ndrangheta, even in this sector, has become a sought-after interlocutor—rather than a threat—for the entrepreneurial world.

Operation Gambling[24] provides another prominent example of the clans' involvement in the gaming industry. As reminded also in Chap. 4, the operation led to the arrest of 41 people and to seizures for a total value of 2 billion euros by dismantling a major illegal system of money laundering operations tracked down in Malta, Panama, Romania, Spain, Serbia, and the Netherland Antilles. The system was run through online casinos by the company Betriq, initially based in Veneto and then in Malta. Servers to manage gambling websites (.com) and to collect revenues were located abroad to bypass Italian laws. What emerges, as clearly stated in the court order, is a situation

> Totally innovative, for what regards the issues under investigation and the outcomes, and at the same time absolutely traditionalist, as it is centred around [...] the 'ndrangheta, which pervades and characterises the social, economic, entrepreneurial, and (sub) cultural texture of the local, national, and [...] international territory.[25]

The Roles of the Clans in the Exploitation of Migrants

Southern Italy, because of its geographical location, has seen over the past few years an unprecedented number of people arriving from poorer and conflict-torn countries, with a steady increase of refugees arriving by sea, for a total of 153,850 in 2015 alone, 29,437 of which disembarked in Calabria (UNHCR 2015). While most part of the smuggling of migrants is not controlled by the clans but rather by other criminal organisations (DNA 2015), 'ndrangheta clans have demonstrated once again to be good partners in crime with their ability to make the most of any opportunity for profits, regardless of the issues at stake, and thanks to the control of their own territories.

Already in 2010, Operation Leone[26] shed light on the involvement of the clans Cordì from Locri and Iamonte from Melito Porto Salvo, near

Reggio Calabria, together with Indian nationals in smuggling 480 illegal workers from India and Pakistan towards Italy, for a total reported
turnover of more than 6 million euros. Every migrant was worth up to
18,000 euros, in a sophisticated mechanism that allowed to facilitate illegal migration through crooked and intimidated employers presenting fake
requests to have a certain numbers of workers from abroad. More recently,
in the context of the investigations for Mafia Capitale in Rome, Operation
"Mondo di Mezzo",[27] it was unpacked and clarified how the clans in
Rome, together with 'ndrangheta clans, managed the immigrant flows
and specifically their accommodation and temporary assistance through
a criminal business developed thanks to public money. As reported by
Rinaldi (2016), an agreement was in place between some actors from
Mafia Capitale and 'ndrangheta affiliated from the Mancuso clan from
Limbadi, near Vibo Valentia—also one of the major clans involved in the
cocaine trafficking through Gioia Tauro—to maximise profits that, as
emerging from wiretappings, were so valuable to be comparable to those
of drugs trafficking in Roma. Once again, the commonality of interests
makes the clans willing to collaborate with other criminal forces. Also, as
revealed in the intercepted materials for Mafia Capitale, the reputation
of the Calabrian clans makes them sought-after partners for other criminal networks, and their pervasiveness in the Calabrian territory is useful
to manage the logistic of criminal activities. Salvatore Buzzi, one of the
alleged bosses of Mafia Capitale, is thankful to Massimo Carminati, the
other alleged boss, for the help with the refugees' camp and its discretion.
He says[28]:

> Massimo is great, he doesn't talk, he talks so little, he says "the less you
> know, the less you talk, the less you know, the safer you are" [...] this is how
> they do it in Calabria [...] you have to know as little as possible.

The relationship between the criminal network in Rome and the
Calabrian clans for the purposes of sharing profits in the cooperatives providing shelter to refugees is based on the political reach recognised to the
Calabrians also beyond Calabria. As said again by Salvatore Buzzi[29] during
an intercepted conversation about political support to a local politician:

> Give him the name or 7–8 people, '*ndranghetisti* we have in our coopera-
> tives [...] just give him the names of these *mafiosi*, they control the votes,
> don't they, you can't get it wrong.

Moreover, ongoing investigations suggest how some of the immigrants once arrived on the Calabrian shores are then exploited through a gangmaster system (*caporalato*)—that is, the activity of unlawful brokerage between employers and workers, which results in the exploitation of illegal work—in the farming industry and in the food distribution markets run by the clans for porterage services (Rinaldi 2016). Therefore, in order to increase their profits by saving money on the workforce, the 'ndrangheta clans and their reputation might have a role in facilitating illegal immigration in Calabria or through Calabria, taking advantage of the desperation of refugees and economic migrants. Indeed, the exploitation of migrants in the region is not new: in 2010, national and international news covered the events related to (often illegal) migrant workers brought into the region for seasonal agricultural work who started to protest against their dramatic life conditions and the racist aggressions they were forced to endure in Rosarno near Gioia Tauro and in between the provinces of Reggio Calabria and Vibo Valentia (Donadio 2010; Stopndrangheta.it and Associazione da Sud 2010).

CONCLUSION

This chapter presented an overview of some core or otherwise relevant activities carried out by the Calabrian clans. Indeed, while most international attention so far has been understandably focused on the role of the 'ndrangheta in cross-border drug trafficking, it is worth noting that many 'ndrangheta clans act as poly-crime networks, which efficiently distribute their risks and maximise their profits through a much wider range of criminal activities, with money and power being the ultimate aims.

Furthermore, from the case studies presented, it emerges once again that even if the clans are highly effective in managing the trans-regional dimension of their businesses and in taking advantage of legal loopholes and permeable borders, their local dimension remains fundamental in understanding their success. Without their participation into the entrepreneurial and political worlds in Calabria, their prosperity would be severely undermined. Through their firm hold on local politics and economics and their strategic activities to control the territory, the clans have successfully reinforced their reputation also beyond the regional borders as reliable partners for other criminal groups in different types of criminal ventures. This successful homogeneous process of '*ndranghetisation* also implies that the 'ndrangheta clans are able to adapt, whenever necessary. After all, this is the real power of that *glocalism* that the clans embraced so well: the traditional mafia method through the explicit use of violence is used only in exceptional cases; the 'ndrangheta intimidates much more subtly by relying on reputation and consolidated behaviours. The new generations of *'ndranghetisti* are open to use new technologies, they are capable businessmen, and can be part of the same elite networks they interact with for their businesses. This is a new way of *being* and *doing* mafia, where 'ndrangheta operations are increasingly normalised in society through accepted corruptive practices, such as in the Mafia Capitale case, and are not anymore confined to Calabrian borders.

NOTES

1. Operation Black Mountains, No. 1138/99 R.G.N.R. DDA.
2. Operation Rifiuti Spa I, No. 5988/06 R.G.N.R. DDA.
3. Operation Rifiuti Spa II, No. 2855/06 R.G.N.R. DDA.
4. Operation Black Mountains, No. 1138/99 R.G.N.R. DDA.
5. Operation Cerberus, No. 30500/04 R.G.N.R. DDA + No. 27453/08 R.G.N.R. DDA.
6. Operation Isola, No.10354/05 R.G.N.R. DDA + No. 2810/05 R.G. GIP.
7. Operation Parco Sud I, No. 41849/07 R.G.N.R. DDA + No. 8183/07 R.G.GIP and Operation Parco Sud II, No. 4458/10 R.G.N.R. DDA + No. 1035/10 R.G.GIP.
8. Operation Tenacia, No. 47816/08 R.G.N.R. DDA.
9. Operation Redux-Caposaldo, No. 37625/08 R.G.N.R. DDA + 32238/09 R.G.N.R. DDA, No. 9189/09 R.G.GIP.
10. Operation Redux-Caposaldo, No. 37625/08 R.G.N.R. DDA + 32238/09 R.G.N.R. DDA No. 9189/09 R.G.GIP.
11. Operation Isola, No.10354/05 R.G.N.R. DDA + No. 2810/05 R.G.GIP.
12. Interview in Catanzaro, DDA Procura della Repubblica, 15 December 2015, translated from Italian.
13. Operation Araba Fenice, sentence No. 311/06 R.G. Court of Appeal Bari.
14. Operation Reggio Sud, No. 80/10 R.G.N.R. DDA.
15. Operation Sistema-Assenzio 4614/06 R.G.N.R. DDA RC + No. 3470/07 R.G.N.R. GIP.
16. Operation Sistema-Assenzio, No. 4614/06 RGNR DDA RC + No. 3470/07 R GIP, p. 87.
17. Operation Acero, No. 7428/2010 R.G.N.R. DDA.
18. Operation Krupy, No. 57055/12 R.G.N.R. DDA.
19. Operation Krupy, No. 57055/12 R.G.N.R. DDA.
20. Operation Acero, No. 7428/2010 R.G.N.R. DDA.
21. Operation Redux-Caposaldo, No. 37625/08 R.G.N.R. DDA + No. 32238/09 R.G.N.R. DDA + No. 9189/09 R.G.GIP.

22. Operation Famiglia Valle, N. 46229/08 R.G.N.R. DDA + No 10464/08 R.G.GIP.
23. Operation Black Monkey, No. 599/10 R.G.N.R. + No. 482/11 R.G. G.I.P. DDA.
24. Operation Gambling, No. 7497/2014 R.G.N.R. DDA +. No. 1609/2015 R.G.GIP.
25. Operation Gambling, No. 7497/2014 R.G.N.R. DDA+ No. 1609/2015 R.G., p. 46.
26. Operation Leone, No. 3994/07 R.G.N.R. DDA.
27. Operation Mondo di Mezzo, No. 30456/10 R.G.N.R. DDA.
28. Operation Mondo di Mezzo, No. 30456/10 R.G.N.R. DDA, p. 774.
29. Operation Mondo di Mezzo, No. 30456/10 R.G.N.R. DDA, p. 316.

REFERENCES

Annibaldi, P., & Tocco, M. (2010). *L'infiltrazione della criminalità organizzata nell'economia di alcune regioni del Nord Italia.* Roma: CNEL.

Arlacchi, P. (1986). *Mafia Business: Mafia ethic and the spirit of capitalism.* London: Verso.

Caneppele, S., Riccardi, M., & Standridge, P. (2013). Green Energy and Black Economy: Mafia Investments in the Wind Power Sector in Italy. *Crime, Law and Social Change, 59*(3), 319–339.

Chiavari, M. (2011). *La quinta mafia. Come e perché la mafia al Nord oggie fatta anche da uomini del Nord.* Milan: Salani.

CNEL. (2012). *Analisi dei rischi di illegalità e penetrazione della criminalità organizzata nel settore dell'energia eolica in Italia.* Roma: Consiglio Nazionale dell'Economia e del Lavoro.

Commissione di Accesso. (2012). *Relazione,* Comune di Reggio Calabria. Roma: Commissione di Accesso al Comune di Reggio Calabria ex art. 143 d.lgs 267/2000.

Commissione Parlamentare d'Inchiesta; (2012). *Relazione territoriale sulle attività illecite connesse al ciclo dei rifiuti nella regione Lombardia.* Roma: Camera dei Deputati, Senato della Repubblica.

Commissione Parlamentare di Inchiesta. (1999). *Commissione Parlamentare di Inchiesta sul ciclo dei rifiuti e sulle attività illecite ad esso connesse. Relazione territoriale sulla Lombardia. XIII Legislatura doc XXIII n.39.,* Roma: Camera dei Deputati, Senato della Repubblica.

Commissione Parlamentare di Inchiesta. (2000a). *Commissione Parlamentare di Inchiesta sul ciclo dei rifiuti e sulle attività illecite ad esso connesse. Documento sui traffici illeciti e le ecomafie. XIII Legislatura, doc XXIII n. 47.,* Roma: Camera dei Deputati, Senato della Repubblica.

Commissione Parlamentare di Inchiesta. (2000b). *Commissione Parlamentare di Inchiesta sul ciclo dei rifiuti e sulle attività illecite ad esso connesse. Relazione*

108   A. SERGI AND A. LAVORGNA

territoriale sulla Calabria. XIII Legislatura, doc XXIII n. 38. Roma: Camera dei Deputati, Senato della Repubblica.

Commissione Parlamentare di Inchiesta. (2011). *Commissione Parlamentare di Inchiesta sulle attivita' illecite connesse al ciclo dei rifiuti. Relazione territoriale sulle attivita' illecite connesse al ciclo dei rifiuti nella regione Calabria. XVI legislatura, doc XXIII n.7.* Roma: Camera dei Deputati, Senato della Repubblica.

CROSS. (2015). *Secondo rapporto trimestrale sulle aree settentrionali per la Presidenza della Commissione Parlamentare di Inchiesta sul fenomeno mafioso.* Milano: Università degli Studi di Milano.

DIA. (2008). *Attività Svolta e Risultati Conseguiti dalla Direzione Investigativa Antimafia, Luglio-Dicembre 2012.* Roma Direzione Investigativa Antimafia: Relazione del Ministro dell'Interno al Parlamento.

DNA. (2012). *Relazione annuale sulle attività svolte dal Procuratore Nazionale Antimafia e dalla Direzione Nazionale Antimafia nonché sulle dinamiche e strategie della criminalità organizzata di tipo mafioso.* Roma: Direzione Nazionale Antimafia.

DNA. (2014). *Relazione annuale sulle attività svolte dal Procuratore Nazionale Antimafia e dalla Direzione Nazionale Antimafia nonché sulle dinamiche e strategie della criminalità organizzata di tipo mafioso.* Roma: Direzione Nazionale Antimafia.

DNA. (2015). *Relazione annuale sulle attività svolte dal Procuratore Nazionale Antimafia e dalla Direzione Nazionale Antimafia nonché sulle dinamiche e strategie della criminalità organizzata di tipo mafioso.* Roma: Direzione Nazionale Antimafia.

DNA. (2016). *Relazione annuale sulle attività svolte dal Procuratore nazionale e dalla Direzione nazionale antimafia e antiterrorismo nonché sulle dinamiche e strategie della criminalità organizzata di tipo mafioso.* Roma: Direzione Nazionale Antimafia e Antiterrorismo.

Donadio, R. (2010, January 10). Race Riots Grip Italian Town, and Mafia Is Suspected. *The New York Times.* http://www.nytimes.com/2010/01/11/world/europe/11italy.html?_r=1.

EU Committee on Civil Liberties. (2010). Fact-Finding Mission ROSARNO and ROME 15–17 February 2010. In: European Parliament, *Justice and Home Affairs.* Brussels: http://www.europarl.europa.eu/document/activities/cont/201003/20100308ATT70139/20100308ATT70139EN.pdf

Eurispes. (2015). Agromafie. 3° Rapporto sui crimini agroalimentari in Italia 2015. *Rapporti Eurispes.* Roma.

Lavorgna, A. (2015a). Dirty business: Italy cracks down on environmental crime. *Jane's Intelligence Review* June, pp. 42–45

Lavorgna, A. (2015b). Organised crime goes online: Realities and challenges. *Journal of Money Laundering Control, 18*(2), 153–168.

Lavorgna, A., & Sergi, A. (2014). Types of organised crime in Italy. The multifaceted spectrum of Italian criminal associations and their different attitudes in the financial crisis and in the use of Internet technologies. *International Journal of Law, Crime and Justice, 42*(1), 16–32.

Legambiente. (2014). *Ecomafia 2014: Nomi e numeri dell'illegalità ambientale.* Milan: Edizioni Ambiente.

Legambiente. (2015). *Ecomafia 2015. Corrotti, clan e inquinatori. I ladri di futuro all'assalto del belpaese,* Napoli: Marotta e Cafiero Editori.

Legambiente. (2016). Ecomafia. http://www.legambiente.it/temi/eco- mafia.

Lupo, S. (2009). *History of the mafia.* New York, Chichester: Columbia University Press.

Open Coesione. (2016). *Regione Calabria. Tutti I progetti,* Interactive Portal available at http://www.opencoesione.gov.it/.

Pergolizzi, A. (2012). *Toxicitaly. Ecomafie e capitalismo: gli affari sporchi all'ombra del progresso.* Rome: Castelvecchi.

Pracchi, C., Colotta, G., Valsecchi, P., et al. (2012). Ecomafie in Italia: una panoramica. *SCORE—Stop Crimes on Renewables and Environment.* Available at http://www.euscore.eu/download.aspx.

Rege, A., & Lavorgna, A. (2016). Organization, operations, and success of environmental organized crime in Italy and India: A comparative analysis. *The European Journal of Criminology.* doi:10.1177/1477370816649627.

Rinaldi, L. (2016). Così i migranti diventano schiavi della 'ndrangheta. Dai Cie al facchinaggio agli ortmercati. Così le 'ndrine fanno profitti sui migranti. La pista del traffico di essere umani. *Linkiesta.it.* http://www.linkiesta.it/it/article/2016/02/05/cosi-i-migranti-diventano-schiavi-della-ndrangheta/29133/.

Ruggiero, V., & South, N. (2010). Green criminology and dirty collar crime. *Critical Criminology, 18,* 251–262.

Sciarrone, R. (2001). E la mafia, starà a guardare? Il rischio criminalità. *Meridiana. Rivista di Storia e Scienze Sociali, 41,* 165–185.

Sergi, A., & Lavorgna, A. (2012). Trade Secrets: Italian Mafia Expands its Illicit Business. *Jane's Intelligence Review,* September

Sergi, A. and South, N. (2016). "Earth, Water, Air, and Fire". Environmental Crimes, Mafia Power and Political Negligence in Calabria. In: G. Antonopoulos (ed.), *Illegal Entrepreneurship, Organised Crime and Social Control: Essays in Honour of Prof. Dick Hobbs.* New York: Springer.

SOS Impresa. (2011). I giochi delle mafie. In: SOS Impresa-Confesercenti, *Rapporti.* http://www.sosimpresa.it/userFiles/File/Documenti4/audizione_cnel_giochi_maggio_2011.pdf

SOS Impresa. (2012). *XIII Rapporto. Le mani della criminalità sulle imprese.,* Rome.

Stopndrangheta.it and Associazione da Sud. (2010). Arance Insanguinate. Dossier Rosarno. http://www.stopndrangheta.it/file/stopndrangheta_875.pdf.

Toscano, P. (2008). L'assessore il garante delle cosche? *Gazzetta del Sud.* 14 February 2008: page 11.

UNHCR. (2015). Italy-UNHCR response to sea arrivals. In: UNHRC (ed). https://data.unhcr.org/mediterranean/download.php?id=528

CHAPTER 7

Conclusion

Abstract This final chapter of the book will draw together the conclusions of our work as presented in the previous chapters. By looking again at the 'ndrangheta as behavioural model spreading through a *'ndranghetisation* process, we pinpoint the main concepts of this book and we review our findings. We also briefly highlight some areas of research and analysis on the 'ndrangheta that this book has not touched upon and identify venues and patterns for further research.

Keywords 'Ndranghetisation • 'Ndranghetism • Mafia Behaviours • Future Research • Limitations

Throughout this book, we have presented the Calabrian mafia, known with the collective name 'ndrangheta, through different lenses. We have used judicial documents and court orders to present a criminological study on the Calabrian clans focused on both their structures and their activities. We have started by looking at the relationship between Calabria and the 'ndrangheta and we have taken the reader on a journey across Italian regions and countries around the world, across transnational criminal markets—such as the cocaine trade—and then back again to local and national criminal activities. We have presented the 'ndrangheta clans as social forces, driven by opportunities for profits as well as nurturing relationships with legal actors, namely politicians and entrepreneurs.

© The Editor(s) (if applicable) and The Author(s) 2016   111
A. Sergi, A. Lavorgna, *'Ndrangheta,*
DOI 10.1007/978-3-319-32585-9_7

Throughout the book, we have kept the focus on three main points. First, as anticipated in the introduction to this book, the 'ndrangheta is a plural phenomenon, there are various *'ndranghete* in Calabria and outside Calabria. Second, the name 'ndrangheta works as a brand name: not only does it refer to a specific criminal organisation with a unitary coordination structure in the hinterland and city of Reggio Calabria but also to a *behavioural model—'ndranghetism*—a set of behaviours adopted by various criminal groups across Calabria and outside the region. In an attempt to simplify even more, we can affirm that 'ndrangheta is the way to *do mafia* in Calabria, where by "mafia" we mean the systematic exploitation of shared cultural values and relationships through the use of usurpation, arrogance, *hubris*, intimidation, violence, and subjection, while also engaging in illegal activities for profit. Moreover, the *'ndranghetism*—the set of mafia-style behaviours adopted by the clans—is made more efficient by the ability of different clans to establish themselves as reliable partners for other criminal and legal entrepreneurs beyond Calabria and at times beyond Italy. Essentially, more than just a mafia-style behaviour, the *'ndranghetism* is the Calabrian innovative way of *being* and *doing* mafia through a dense network of relationships (also because of massive migration from Calabria), both in the upperworld and in the underworld, a particularly acute sense of business, a reputation built on the protection of blood and family ties, and, last but not least, the symbiotic relationship and the camouflage within Calabrian society. Third, the more the behavioural model has become homogeneous, the more the process of *'ndranghetisation* has been reinforced by the reputation of the clans. Today various groups are associated to, and branded with, an idea of 'ndrangheta as a unique and criminal organisation when links with Calabrian criminals are found. While some clans in Calabria act under the same coordination structures and others on a looser basis, the *'ndranghetisation* process is based on the behavioural model that all clans share.

In this book, we have presented the 'ndrangheta clans and their behaviours by focusing specifically on their organisational skills, their bonds with the Calabrian society and also with Calabrian communities outside the region, their mobility, and their characterisation as poly-crime networks. All data and the cases presented throughout the book need to be interpreted together: there is no division between what the 'ndrangheta clans *are* and what they *do*. The structural composition of the clans, both in regional and in extra-regional settings, is functional to the successful engagement in illegal activities: what characterise the Calabrian clans is not only flexibility of roles and business acumen, but also the ability to move money, goods, and people quickly while at the same time securing immunity from prosecution and escaping detection.

The title of this book, as already pointed out in the introduction chapter, is critical. In our understanding of the phenomenon of the 'ndrangheta, as said, the Calabrian region plays an essential role. Everything starts and ends in Calabria, even when the core of illegal activities and profits is elsewhere. We have argued that the 'ndrangheta clans need to be static to be dynamic: they need the local roots to expand nationally and globally; they certainly need for Calabria to remain the underdeveloped, underachieving region that it unfortunately is. Only by controlling economic and political processes in the region of Calabria the clans, the most successful ones at least, can step into the national and international arena. Coming back to the title, therefore, we can affirm that when the authorities dub the 'ndrangheta as the *most powerful* Italian mafia, they do not only refer to the clans' involvement in illegal activities worldwide and the nature of their profits, which are allegedly higher than other criminal groups. The 'ndrangheta is indeed the most powerful Italian mafia because it is the most local and the most global at the same time, it is successfully *glocal*. The traditional core of the basic organisational structure of the 'ndrangheta—the family-based *'ndrine*—is grounded on the respect and enforcement of those shared social and cultural values of the Calabrian community and it is the springboard to reach out for markets and opportunities outside the *'ndrine* and their territories.

Calabria has always been the cradle for the clans. It was 1975 when, during a maxi-trial against 60 clan members (when the law still did not recognise the mafia membership offence), a judge identified in the sentence the so-called Rischio Calabria—Calabrian Risk—by quantifying that the costs of any investment in the region were systematically inflated by 15 %—that is, the estimated cost of mafia interference (Sergi 1991: 91). The "Calabrian Risk"—the consideration that in Calabrian economy mafia presence has a *cost*—is not an obsolete concept, as it is still the reality of Calabrian economy and it is now exported also outside regional boundaries. Because of that, we argue that a proper understanding of the 'ndrangheta cannot occur without knowledge of Calabrian society, politics, and economy. This knowledge is also necessary to avoid the cultural stereotypes, which worry authorities in non-traditional mafia settlements, unwilling, and rightfully so, to openly connect mafia presence with people having Calabrian origins fearing racist allegations. Certainly, it is crucial to avoid these stereotypes, as culture is not an indicator of mafia's birth and evolution. However, it is equally fundamental to understand how in Calabria cultural elements have been twisted in support of social promotion and profit orientation when the structural weaknesses of the territory allow an easier disregard for regulations and an easier entry or disguise into certain sectors through illegal means.

By the end of this book, the reader should be left with an understanding not only of what it means for the Calabrian mafia to have evolved symbiotically within Calabrian society, but also of how this evolution is mirrored in the fragmented nature of the 'ndrangheta. Whenever news of the 'ndrangheta hit the general public, from Italy or worldwide, the reader should always ask "which 'ndrangheta?". The manifestations of the Calabrian clans always need to be unpacked by analysing their actual links with the territory when in Calabria or their communication with their homeland if outside Calabria. Otherwise, the risk is to simplify the phenomenon as a singular one (*la*—the—'ndrangheta) by reducing it to something that does not match the very multifaceted and composite reality of the Calabrian clans in Calabria, Italy, and abroad, their autonomy and their flexibility.

While this book has been concerned about describing the 'ndrangheta phenomenon through the most recent and the most important investigations carried out by Antimafia prosecutors, we are very conscious of the limits of our analysis. The most significant limit of our book is probably the lack of consideration of the reactions of civil society to the clans' presence in Calabria and elsewhere. We certainly do not forget that mafia affiliates are individuals with their own families and social relationships and therefore the criminal phenomenon is always intertwined with society at large in Calabria as elsewhere, by consensus as well as by subjugation. Academic literature on the social perceptions of the 'ndrangheta is very thin (Neubacher 2013; Allum 2013; Pratticò 2014), while reviews of social reactions and interpretations of the 'ndrangheta phenomenon among Calabrian citizens and immigrants are usually limited to journalistic efforts (Reski 2012; Forgione 2012). Analyses of anti-mafia movements against the 'ndrangheta are also limited (Cayli 2013; Mattoni 2013). In Calabria, it is not easy to discuss certain topics openly, as intimidation, *omertà*, and fear of retaliation are indeed part of the territorial control enforced by the clans. In addition, problems with the denial of the 'ndrangheta by some people in Calabria or by migrated Calabrian communities can also be considered a sign of blindness due to their over-exposure to the phenomenon.

We have not touched upon these issues in length in our work, as our focus was mostly on the criminals and their activities, rather than on their impact and harm to societies.

In addition, we have not lingered extensively on the policing of the 'ndrangheta and on the judicial difficulties in investigating and prosecuting the clans. These difficulties are not only due to problems of *omertà* and/or intimidation within and outside Calabria, but are also due to the technical issues that arise in pigeonholing certain 'ndrangheta-related criminal networks and activities as "mafia" according to article 416-*bis* of the Criminal Code (DNA 2015; Lavorgna and Sergi 2014; Dalla Chiesa 2015; Sergi 2016). In fact, as briefly explained in Chap. 3, especially in situations of delocalisation, when there is not a clear link between the actions of the clans and the condition of subjugation of communities, the *'ndranghetist behaviour* manifests itself in more subtle ways. This might mean that the legal requirements to qualify the criminal actors involved as parts of a mafia-type criminal association might not be easily met.

Another interesting aspect in the study of the 'ndrangheta is the role of women in 'ndrangheta families and in criminal activities of the clans. The 'ndrangheta has showed a very different approach than other mafia groups to gender in family ranking and affiliations; while affiliation seems to be still officially exclusive to men, this might not have been always the case historically and homogeneously among various clans across Calabria. Often, we have had "sorelle di omertà", *sisters of omertà*, to indicate a recognition of women's roles in the clans (Siebert 2007; Ingrascì 2011). We have seen examples of women running family businesses not out of necessity (for instance, because husbands and sons were in jail) but out of choice, strategy, and charisma (Ingrascì 2007b; Ingrascì 2007a). At the same time, however, women have also been victims of mafia violence and intimidation when willingly or unwillingly sharing the burden of "belonging" to a mafia family (Cerreti 2013). We have not given any voice to these issues throughout our book, even though we consider this as a highly interesting and topical field of research, to be further explored also in relation to the structure and the internal functioning of the clans. However, our book has been more focused on the judicial findings correlated to the label of the 'ndrangheta as the most powerful Italian mafia; the clans, more than single affiliates, have been protagonists. We have left aside a specific analysis of the role of women in 'ndrangheta families, which, we feel, requires an approach more focused on gender and necessarily linked to individual experiences and case studies.

This book also overlooked the rituals of affiliation and the codes of honour and violence that regulate clans and interactions among clans in the recruitment and management of affiliates (Ciconte 2015). We certainly recognise the importance of codes of rituals and their symbolism, as they confirm the traditional character of the 'ndrangheta as culturally linked to the territory of Calabria and as experience of social bonding and collective narcissism. However, we could only briefly refer to the existence of such codes in our text, because, again, we have been concerned with an analysis of judicial evidence rooted in historical findings of both the local and the global dimension of the clans. An analysis of codes and rituals of affiliations, the symbolism of formulas and oaths, would be more appropriate for an anthropological study, which this book could not engage with.

Last but not least, this book could not address all the activities where the clans are deemed to be active and some significant ones had to be neglected or only briefly mentioned, such as, for example, extortion, usury, and counterfeiting. However, the broad and diverse range of activities selected for the analysis should give our readers a good overview of the extreme ability of the clans to "seize the opportunity" and to diversify their revenue streams, both locally and internationally. Once again, it is worth noting that even if the clans can and do *go global*, the key to their success and their pervasiveness is to be found in their homeland, their ability to innovate and to move in new crime domains in their strict control of their traditions.

We hope that the analysis of the 'ndrangheta and of the *'ndraghetisation* processes offered in this book can stimulate further research in this domain in order to explore and explain with academic rigour the aspects we could not linger on, and many more.

Overall, the situation described by this book does not leave much room to optimism. The clans are strong, as well established is their *modus agendi*. The structural weaknesses they exploit are not easy to tackle. The clans can take advantage of their power of intimidation, their reputation, as well as the collusive behaviours of some of their supporters. However, the success of recent law enforcement operations and especially the Antimafia's capacity to shed some light on key aspects of the 'ndrangheta and *'ndranghetism* give some hope. A better understanding of the phenomenon by the general public and an effort towards *responsibilisation* of the political and business elites in Italy and beyond are nonetheless necessary steps for a prompt reaction and an effective immunisation towards the clans.

We finally wish to remind the readers that even though media, judicial, and scholarly attention to the phenomenon of the 'ndrangheta can superficially shed negative light on the people and places of Calabria, knowledge and accuracy in analysis of the mafia phenomenon are necessary to make sure that Calabria is not further discriminated upon and its citizens not labelled or misunderstood.

REFERENCES

Allum, F. (2013). Padrini, occhiali scuri e pasta: percezioni inglesi delle mafie italiane. *Sicurezza e scienze sociali*, *3*, 55–73.

Cayli, B. (2013). Italian civil society against the Mafia: From perceptions to expectations. *International Journal of Law, Crime and Justice*, *41*(1), 81–99.

Cerreti, A. (2013). Il coraggio della verità. In: E. Ciconte, F. Forgione, and I. Sales (eds) *Atlante delle Mafie. Storia, economia, società, cultura. Volume II*. Soveria Mannelli: Rubbettino.

Ciconte, E. (2015). *Riti criminali. I codici di affiliazione alla 'ndrangheta*. Soveria Mannelli: Rubbettino.

Dalla Chiesa, N. (2015). A proposito di Mafia Capitale. Alcuni Problemi Teorici. *CROSS. Rivista di Studi e Ricerche sulla Criminalità Organizzata*, *1*(2): DOI: 10.13130/cross-16634.

DNA. (2015). *Relazione annuale sulle attività svolte dal Procuratore Nazionale Antimafia e dalla Direzione Nazionale Antimafia nonché sulle dinamiche e strategie della criminalità organizzata di tipo mafioso*. Rome: Direzione Nazionale Antimafia.

Forgione, F. (2012). *Porto Franco. Politici, Manager e Spioni nella Repubblica della 'Ndrangheta*. Milan: Dalai Editore.

Ingrascì, O. (2007a). *Donne d'onore. Storie di mafia al femminile*. Milano: Mondadori.

Ingrascì, O. (2007b). Women in the 'Ndrangheta: the Serraino-Di Giovine case. In G. Fiandaca (Ed.), *Women and the Mafia*. New York: Springer.

Ingrascì, O. (2011). Donne, 'ndrangheta, 'ndrine. Gli spazi femminili nelle fonti giudiziarie. *Meridiana. Rivista di Storia e Scienze Sociali*, *67*, 35–54.

Lavorgna, A., & Sergi, A. (2014). Types of organised crime in Italy. The multifaceted spectrum of Italian criminal associations and their different attitudes in the financial crisis and in the use of Internet technologies. *International Journal of Law, Crime and Justice*, *42*(1), 16–32.

Mattoni, A. (2013). I movimenti antimafie in Italia. In: E. Ciconte, F. Forgione, and I. Sales (eds) *Atlante delle Mafie. Storia, economia, società, cultura. Volume II*. Soveria Mannelli: Rubbettino.

Neubacher, F. (2013). Le mafie italiane, percezione del fenomeno in Germania. *Sicurezza e scienze sociali, 3*, 33.54.

Pratticò, N. (2014). La mafia al nord. Dal negazionismo alla presa di coscienza dell'esistenza del fenomenonelle forme della colonizzazione e delocalizzazione. *Questione Giustizia*, 207–221.

Reski, P. (2012). *The honoured society: the secret history of Italy's most powerful Mafia*. London: Atlantic.

Sergi, A. (2016c). A proposito di Mafia Capitale. Spunti per tipizzare il fenomeno mafioso nei sistemi di common law". *Rivista di Studi e Ricerche sulla criminalità organizzata, 2*(1), 96–116. Open Access http://riviste.unimi.it/index.php/cross/article/view/6974.

Sergi, P. (1991). *La "Santa" Violenta*. Cosenza: Periferia.

Siebert, R. (2007). *Mafia women: The affirmation of a female pseudo-subject, the case of the 'Ndrangheta*. New York: Springer.

INDEX

© The Editor(s) (if applicable) and The Author(s) 2016
A. Sergi, A. Lavorgna, *Ndrangheta*,
DOI 10.1007/978-3-319-32585-9

119

Printed by Printforce, the Netherlands